CREATED REALITIES

JEAN-YVES SOLINGA

FIRST EDITION

Little Red Tree Publishing, LLC,
509 W 3rd Street, North Platte, NE 69101

Layout and Cover Design: Michael Linnard, MCSD
Times New Roman, Trajan Pro and Ariel.

First Edition, 2017, manufactured in USA
1 2 3 4 5 6 7 8 9 10   LSI   23 22 21 20 19 18 17

"Birth of a Muse," page 44, and "Waking up in Saint Germain des prés," page 86, first appeared in *Peacock Journal Anthology: Beauty First*, Vol 1, No 2., July 2017.

Photograph on page 113 by Andrea Keller.

Photograph on page x by Elaine Solinga.

Library of Congress Cataloging-in-Publication Data

Names: Solinga. Jean-Yves, author.
Title: Created Realities/ by Jean-Yves Solinga
Description: First edition. | North Platte, NE : Little Red Tree
  Publishing, 2017. | Includes index.
Identifiers: LCCN 2017027852 | ISBN 9781935656517 (pbk. : alk. paper)
Subjects: LCSH: Poetry
Classification: LCC PS3573.I4787 A6 2017 | DDC 811/.54--dc23
LC record available at https://lccn.loc.gov/2017027852

Little Red Tree Publishing LLC
509 W 3rd Street,
North Platte, NE 69101
www.littleredtree.com

Contents

FOREWORD

Late 2015 I relocated to Nebraska. My wife and I found a beautiful Arts and Craft house in North Platte, the home of Buffalo Bill Cody and the Union Pacific Railway's marshalling yard, the biggest in the world, and once settled I continued to publish books.

Having previously published eight books of poetry from Jean-Yves in as many years it wasn't long before reports of a ninth were beginning to reach me. In due course the manuscript of *Creating Realities* appeared in my inbox.

Consequently, I am yet again presented with the task of writing a foreword in response to another collection of poems from my friend Jean-Yves Solinga, a task I take great pride in performing. In this book, Jean-Yves revisits the fundamental issue of "reality" as created by the artist from fragments of the day-to-day mundane life that we all live and exist within; from pieces of text accidentally read; from long lost memories; from casual conversations or merely witnessed while shopping for tomorrows dinner. The imaginative attenuation between things real and imagined is often microscopically thin but never broken entirely.

Jean-Yves again endlessly explores humanity's perception of reality within an existentialist view of the absurdity of breathtaking beauty and unspeakable horror as they inhabit the same space and time. In his inimitable style of multilayered, multifaceted images his poems bring us both nearer to uncomfortable truths in which most would not willingly venture, or to a point of passion or beauty we could not have previously envisioned.

While most writers wait for the muse to appear or reveal itself to them, to Jean-Yves every memory, event, spoken word, or visual stimulation has significance and potential, requiring an immediate response. Nothing in his stream of consciousness or, in fact, unconsciousness is irrelevant to the process of creating his poetry. And as I have previously noted several times he is prolific and constantly writes. I for one am constantly amazed at his endless imagination and dedication to his craft.

Michael Linnard,
North Platte, NE, 2017

ACKNOWLEDGEMENT

An artist can sometimes feel more at ease in the universe of his art than the reality around his writing table or just outside the window. The energy of the creative activity is fed very often by a jealous demand of concentration: This to the detriment of what exists ten feet away in the kitchen. That is usually good for the art, but less so, for the practicalities of living. The acknowledgment section of a book is the opportunity to bring it back to its elemental blocs and what they signify to the work, the author, and his art.

I owe the availability, the presence of *Created Reality* to Little Red Tree publishing. Michael Linnard has been there for me since *Clair-Obscur of the Soul*; and is once again publishing my work. Michael, in true professional fashion, guided the process of readying the manuscript from its pre-print format, to the printing, and countless changes in between. I want to thank him for his steadfast support and belief in my work and, particularly, for his support of the poetry genre.

I recognize, once more my father Marcel Laurent, my mother, Anna Félicie (née Ciccariello), brother, Pierre Paul and sister Marie Louise Menders for their unconditional love toward me and their family tales of years of Nazi occupation: a setting that helps define the nobility and beauty of human endurance.

To my son, Robert Marcel, his wife Elizabeth and their son Luc. To my daughter Nicole Solinga-Stasi, her husband Marc and their daughters Noëlle and Luciana.

And especially to my wife Elaine, who has gently accepted my hours of immersion and bringing me back to another reality, with whiffs of Poulet à la Marengo and the pop of a blanc de Bourgogne.

Jean-Yves Vincent Solinga
July 2017

On the Seine, facing Notre Dame de Paris.
Photo by Elaine Solinga.

INTRODUCTION

Beauty.

She touches your forehead,
With fingers of cool droplets.
She whispers imagery
Full of the disincarnated presences of the past:
Leaving you panting on your pillow,
Wishing it all had been true. (J-Y.S.)

Artists have had a rich and complicated relationship with their Muse(s). She (if a feminine voice) can be in the forefront: acknowledged and identifiable. For some artists, the identification and the nature of the relationship can be primordial to the body of the poetry [Alfred de Musset and George Sand, come to mind]. But, in any case, these muses have an important part of their entity linked to the surrounding reality (realities) of the artist: which implies that there is a process of absorption between the hard reality and the artist's filtering action for his creative needs. This cross-fertilization has been one of leitmotif of my poetry: with the possible exception of more historically or autobiographically based themes or inspiration [where I still overlap people and settings]. I have, therefore, liberally modified details and references, as to afford me artistic freedom: World War Two based poems during the occupation, are a combination of the different family lore of tales from various neighbors told around the kitchen table and added intermingled details for enrichment; while in university-life based poems, are included, for the most part, observations passively gathered during iconic "bull sessions," after-party "debriefings and unsolicited confessions": which are then remixed for my poetry.

But it is creative freedom that I cherish the most and, for that reason, I have found that *fictionalized reality* (or like the title of this collection *Created Reality*) allows me to use the exhilarating power of a quasi-creator of staged settings. Some are built in the more solid world of realism—less favorable to lyricism—but, even there ["Love… Un-verbalized: a Fable"] humanity always speaks. Poetry has its righteous place in the topics of war, racism, imminent death or the prolonged hunger of children.

There are times in my poetry for the mist of impressionism, the academic angle, or for the inner architectural support of philosophy and thinkers (Camus, Pascal, yes, even Le Marquis de Sade). This mist allows for some interpretation or reconstruction on the reader's part. Indeed, I came across some of my university notes dealing with the hot topic of the times (generally under the heading of *la nouvelle critique*), dealing with the relationship between the writer and the reader, and this note: "Or, pour Barthes, *"l'auteur est mort"*: il affirme que *"la naissance du lecteur doit se payer de la mort de l'auteur"* [Indeed, for Barthes, "the author is dead," he asserts that *"the birth of the reader is at the price of the death of the author."*] Powerful statement!

As for my choice for the epigram of this book, "Madame Bovary, c'est moi." It is eye-catching by its apparent non-nonsensical nature. It is not unlike Roland Barthes' advocacy for the "death of the author." Both of these remarks [it seems to me] deal with the presence or removal of the author [the creator of the text] and her or his leaving behind an unhindered authenticity for literary identity of the voice of the text. That is, indeed, what preoccupies me in several poems. It came to a head when I repeatedly heard echoes of Baudelaire's voice when listening again to Jimi Hendrix's sweet sadness in "Little Wing": How else could the two be related but in the carnal damage that the inherent sensitive talent of a Baudelaire and a Hendrix brought to the search for inspiration; their willing disponibility to the richness of chaos. The author disappearing for having taken the nature [the DNA] of language itself. At times, I wish that we knew even less about the historical Shakespeare: because that would make his words and only his words… ever having had a life.

Paris, southern France, memories of the Maghreb and getting to know American culture, continue to drive my poetry. The harder edges of life and world events ["Charlie Hebdo"], have tried to dry the well that this city represents to me: so far, not successfully. I have kept my word to my desert traveling companion and alter ego "Sidi Moussa": having lost, youth, I kept the passion. ["A Foretaste of America," "The Reality of an Instant."]

I have very slightly re-ordered my poems from their creation; but, generally, kept the effect of the daily stream of consciousness, interests and the variety of themes that my mind brought forth during the writing of the book.

I probably have, for today's Twitter world, an inordinate reverence for words: their meaning, roots, layers of cultural and religious undertones. To my mind, these are important cultural props that accompany creative writing. I like the idea of poems coming to life by their interaction with a knowing public—or that afore-mentioned "reader" of Barthes. My poems, as such, do not strive for the immediacy, the primordial energy of slam poetry: while I am sensitive to the oral genesis of poetry as the original structured oral communication: decibels do not add to my style of writing. My words are constructed to generate mainly power of thought through images and imagery. I take my inspiration from the verbal canvases of Hugo, the landscape echoes of the poetic-prose of the essays of Camus, the knowing feminine sensitivity of Stendhal, the undercurrent sentimentality under the cold light of reality of Flaubert.

Finally, publishing is sharing with a public. This involves a certain tension, a balance, a proportionality between the private, the intimate and degrees of transparency. Not being a non-fiction writer, I have long ago adopted a technique made famous by Proust: the "pastiche." It is the writing equivalent of the artist, in front of the model, mixing colors on the palette to produce something else (i.e. seen and modified through human eyes) or new.

Jean-Yves Vincent Solinga
Gales Ferry, Connecticut 2017

"Madame Bovary… c'est moi" (Gustave Flaubert)

"I am… Madame Bovary"

The Reality of an Instant

Bormes-les-mimosas, France

She had just left his arms,
The pillows
still containing her curves in their shadows.
The merchants
had already stacked the boxes of powdery yellow fluffs on their tri-porters.
Whiffs of shouts and February smells,
seemed to create waves in the cheap curtains.
And he felt a frustrating fear:
a recurring loneliness in his empty embrace:
of knowing that
in a few hours, she would be… both gone… and living eternally
on the rough-textured cellulose of poetry:
protected within curves of black ink.

"Common sense tells us that the things of the earth exist only a little, and that true reality is only in dreams." (Charles Baudelaire)

This comment about reality by a nineteenth century poet, could be relegated to the archives of humanism. And yet, neuro-sciences are finding more evidence of the multi-faceted definition of sight and memory; and thus, of mankind's format of that reality. Starting, decades ago, with how little of the light spectrum we see and the inverted image of the world on the retina. And now, how sight and memory of it, is literally chemically induced and or stored in our fragile brains. What is more real? The recorded passion of a talented (if slightly flawed Parisian poet) or the latest technology that claims to reproduce reality with more pixels and bites?

Death on a Beach

No reprieve from fate.
No benevolence from the puppet masters:
Divine or wood-carvers.

Just the un-appealable simplicity of the death of the innocents.
No whishing stars and splendid fairies.
No divine protection and second chances:
Just real-life monsters.

The limp figurine, with the pinewood heart,
Will remain silent on the sand.

The interaction of the Hellenistic gods,
Hovering over this Mediterranean beach,
Having long ago stopped intervening
In the unjust world of the living.

And it is in a cosmic void,
That fathers… real or otherwise… cry.

Inspired by the eerie similarity in the television footage of the drowned toddler Syrian refugee, off of the coast of Turkey, to the one in the Walt Disney version of the story of Pinocchio, after his escape from Monstro, the whale.

In Lieu of Reality
Part I

A chance re-reading of Baudelaire's "Spleen of Paris" and Jimmy Hendrix's introduction to music and his guitar, prompted the pairing of these two poems. Although insulated from each other in space and time, both artists use the same critical ingredients of personal sensitivity and ambient menacing clouds to share in their reality.

*Homage and credit to Baudelaire and anonymous others
who have loved Paris.*

Walking the Paris streets
with the stray nature of a stray dog.

Sniffing around mounds of detritus of lives and the living
left in the open culverts.

Flesh and stones
cohabiting in a conscious promiscuity:
Invasion of one by the other.

Lucifer himself incapable of returning to his hellish warmth,
Would rather venture among his future mates,
To better enjoy the willingness in humans,

Preparing the damnation of their soul,
By letting the body absorb the luscious slime of happiness.

The artificial having been declared more real than reality:
Opium vapors bellowing dreams of far-way lands,
Made of acrid oils and scented paths.

Of uncovered breasts rivaling the ones in hotel rooms:
Salvation in the arms of old prostitutes' angelic faces.

Adulterated alcohol with after taste of fine champagne.
Young girls in transparent garment with the aura of his catechism days.

Days when a glance of motherly reprimand
meant a day of purgatory.
His feet deep in the filthy urban mud
And his eyes overlooking the vast expanse,

Of what his little boy's heart had always craved:
His salvation… paid in ingots of purity and its weight...
in density of reality.

Access to reality through art.

In Lieu of Reality Part II:
Jimi Hendrix: Little Wing

To the artist... who discerns shreds beauty in our world.

Que tu viennes du ciel ou de l'enfer, qu'importe,
Ô Beauté! monstre énorme, effrayant, ingénu!
Si ton oeil, ton sourire, ton pied... m'ouvrent la porte
D'un Infini que j'aime et nai jamais connu?
("Hymne à la beauté" dans Les fleurs du mal, Charles Baudelaire)

What matter if from hell or heaven born,
Tremendous monster, terrible to view?
Your eyes and smile reveal to me, like morn,
The Infinite I love but never knew.
("Hymn to beauty," Roy Campbell, Poems of Baudelaire)

"Sometimes she [the figure of the feminine ideal for Jimi Hendrix] is a spirit, sometimes a fantasy, sometimes a woman as solidly, palpably physical as he is." (by Music journalist Charles Shear Murray)

Little whispers of her gentle offerings,
Left behind in a self-destructive,
Demonic Baudelairean space of flesh and drugs.

Sensitive soul... survivor in a sharp-edged surrounding:
Grasping at an inner golden ring.

Maybe a broom stick fashioned into a famed guitar neck,
With the emotional weight of a child's Teddy bear?

Blank canvases of sleepless miserable nights:
Building blocks for lyrics and plaintive elasticity of notes.

Surprising classic poetic tonality of sentiments, in this hippieish soul
Attempting to touch the untouchable.

And in the end..
Both artists dying in vapors of opiates and vulgarity of alcohol,

While probably hearing wisps of moments of happiness,
Reconstructed, frisson by nervous frisson, for us...

Secular believers and *disciples of beauty* in the temple of martyrs…
Who otherwise would simply live and die in the solidity of feverish sweat.

Bad boys… grabbing for survival, in the surrounding flesh
And… in the end, left holding a dream…

Still searching for renewal of the spirit
In the perversion found in the rich manure of the misery
Of unfulfilled quest of an ideal.

The rapid dexterity of his fingers on the frets
Like an escapist image full of floral Scandinavian scent,
Where the ears and eyes of artists, are mere organs of reception:

Like these giant cosmic earth-bound sensors,
Concentrating their parabolas on incalculable atoms from eternity.

Giving us pearls…. exquisite organic pearls… of idealized cosmic dust.

Eternal Optimism

Humans… eternally attempting to renew
Eternal illusions of renewed hopes.

Codifying, in the alchemy of words,
A semblance of magic incantations:
Hopefully giving human form to fragile vapors of hope.

Carried within, a protective space… an insulated cocoon…
An inner world for the brittle heart.

Fragile vapors of hope;
And semblance of magic incantations.

Cocoon world of insular glances,
Trying to convince the heart
To enter, once more, the carrousel of flesh.

Strange renewal for a human heart:
Made of the resilient fiber of youth;
Still full of the effervescence of endless hope…

… Some sort of quaint belief… that time is endless;
And the future, safely behind.

We do eventually lose youth... but keep the passion.

Thoughts about the college dating scene: now waiting for new Saturday night date.

Looking for Miracles

Sometimes, an unorthodox language
Speaks for what is good and right.

It is made of gentle ripples
In the green nuances of the side meanders of a river.

Other times, it in the eternal imagery of a nursing mother:
Stirring a fish and vegetable broth.

It is made of the acrid smoke of reed-huts
That define a templar human space.

It will be coming from the first cries
From the entrails of the newly-married village girl.

The seemingly undirected routine of the natural and mundane
Acquiring the nobility of the immortal.

Volumes of geo-politics, studied in academe.
Position papers on Communist domino theory.
Mutual assured destruction.

Burning and smoking flesh from Napalm drops.
Reality of deforestation and pacification,
In the name of abstractions of democracy.

After mankind's best efforts
To destroy a sort of paradisiacal innocence,
Could it be, that the gods in their sorrow, decide once in while,
To let us back… into the Garden?

Inspired by a program on the lyrical serenity of the river villages and the surviving cultures on the Mekong: circa thirty years after the war in Viet Nam.

Galatea Unchained

To Stendhal, whom Simone de Beauvoir, claimed was the only writer to have created true women.

"A certain reserve in her demeanor...
As though she were conscious
Of the danger of letting herself go...
An extraordinary lubricity to safeguard."
("Reserve and Passion," in *Clair-Obscur of the Soul*)

"She was taking possession of him with her stare...
He felt intimidated... as though he were reading his own virility in her eyes."
("Seeing Oneself Being Loved," in *Clair-Obscur of the Soul*)

It was her self-confidence...
In charge of her own destiny.
A finished product, in a world of débutantes:
Appearing, in his soul,
Fully formed... As she came down the stairs.

His mind still whirling with images of academia's Pygmalion
Prisoner of a chisel in masculine hands.

She was the fruit, in an over-picked orchard,
Somehow left untouched, for her not abiding to acceptable standards.

At first... a willful solidity of temperament:
She would eventually offer him precious glimpses of undercurrents of
birdlike fragility
And... finally... an all-defining passion.

Letting his academic universe invade reality...
He had romanticized his expectations,
Passively,
Searching... in the shadows of Thursday-night mixers:
While his classmates expected to make vague memories
of forgettable encounters.

He expected scenes from the shores of Lake Como:
Looking for the mistress of his heart.

Entering the rites of courtship:
Hoping for moments, upon moments of feminine virility.

A feminine void… in him… to match
A masculinity in her soul.

He rightly found an exquisite and yet natural complexity,
In her needs and taste,
That exhibited itself in a disinterest for the mundane of university life.
Thus, creating a surprising aura about her.

He would be allowed to pull back her self-protective sheen,
Discovering in her, a reciprocal body still partially formed:
Waiting for the Other to fill the space.

But time and reality are the death of dreams and dreamers,
And being in love cannot be captured by marble:
The blood of passion wants to coalesce in protective scabs.

And the danger, of bleeding emotionally to death, avoided
By the simplicity of the cellulose of notebooks in the cool corner of a desk.

In love with love: university weekends.

Microbial Thoughts

Of Blaise Pascal's Les deux infinis *(The Two Infinites) and Stephen Hawking's* A Brief History of Time.

Deepest petroleum well:
Its tip, touching dark ooze in the blackness of eons past.

Residue containing organic particles:
Encapsulating prehistoric solar warmth.

Leaves and animal flesh in the giant circle of life and living,
Having given their share back to earth.

All this liquid, full of pageantry and nothingness:
Circling along on its ride with the globe:
Everything... apparently blissfully unaware of itself.

However...
Fables and poetry, contain man-made elementary particles
To create their own universe, made of the power of subjectivity;

Creating intersections, between cosmological mortal enemies,
That are... consciousness and nothingness.

And so... in a sort of literary Genesis...
Let us assume mankind inside that drop of oil, at the bottom of that well.
A minuscule life, capable of great thoughts
—Such as love and the fear of death—

Along with artists, thinkers, and dreamers,
Helping us to bravely project luminous futures, on walls of darkness.

Reflection on Blaise Pascal's glorification of mankind's very consciousness of life itself, and Stephen Hawking's showing us our negligible status in the vastness of space.

Sanctuary City for a Libertine of the Heart

Remark made late at night, on boulevard Saint Germain des Prés, in Paris:
"I authorize this city to give indulgences to illicit lovers."

Privileged places in our world,
Declared such by .... poets and dreamers.
Free thinkers of the heart.

Lovers for the most part… and impatient with commandments:
Not wanting to wait for the good graces of the gods.
And those keepers of time: collaborators with the faculty-room clock.

Places, time and passionate minutes,
that can ultimately make… libertines… out of the best of us.

These very earthy places, with wide boulevards,
Opened to surprisingly romantic gray skies,
Narrow alleys, that smell of furtive embraces;
And squares, full of acrid European tobacco smells.

Flowing water, from street cleaners,
that tempt you to take the next left.
The body, and its sentient soul:
Under the spell of the late hour,
Her floral perfume,
And the warmth of sweat on her lips.

All of the alchemy of this city...
Chosen to be in the middle of a river,
At the bottom of a hill, for deluded future martyrs of religions.

… Makes one, look away from these temporal restrictions,
To instead, quench eternal human thirst.

It is when…
While in the darkness of a corner of a medieval church
—Where one sees dangerous carnal shadows among pious marble—

We deliberately redefine the rules of Hell:
Declaring them soothing… and welcoming.

Making the infernal entrance-fee, the only one, ultimately worth… its price.

Inspired by Adèle's "Someone like you," (the version with the City of Paris as background).

Messages From the Future

Bill Haley and the Comets: "Rock around the clock."

It was not for a lack of music repertoire:
North Africa... Casablanca... Meknès... Fez... Tanger!

Incestuous cohabitations:
of rhythmic Sahel tam-tams,
hypnotic flutes and off-beat clapping, in *bled*,
olive-grove imagery, from Andalusian sounds from taverns,
lyrical accordion melodies, capturing latest Parisian side-walk scenery.

And then...
... in the darkness of the local cinema... Le Fantasio,
before the main picture... mixed with Bazooka aroma on the tongue...

... a cacophony of twisting bodies,
explosions of sounds...

And a beat... a driving, alien beat...

Pleasantly confusing... mesmerizing... to a pubescent mind and eyes:
As though the screen had send out coded truths from the future.

Introduction to American culture through the pre-feature, newsreel section in a North Africa movie-house, circa 1950's.

More Real Than Reality

The power of fiction

Introductory intimacies with fiction:
The dreaded high school English class assignment,
Interpreted, at first, as sadistic interference with week-end plans:

At other times, late night reading under the warmth of bedspread:
maybe on a "dark and windy night."

Or maybe, an early sensual thought upon reading what seems to be
a perfect author's description of the eyes of the girl in algebra class.

Maybe, an eerie similarity of an early nineteenth century conversation
with the one overheard between parents in the kitchen.

Maybe, an uncanny similarity with the stubborn acme condition
And the social rejection of the story's heroine.

Fantastically alien situations, made of such plasticity,
That only the complicity of the reader can accommodate the mind of the writer.

This quasi-divine power of the artist... the writer
akin to the index of God.

Parallel worlds, of limitless expansion,
Opening at the rate of the cursor on the screen.

Thus, for the creation of Jean Valjean and Atticus Finch,
In the primordial soup of fiction,
Found between the granite of Paris and humidity of Alabama.

The "literary persona" of Jean Valjean, from the mind of Victor Hugo, could not be anything short of a secular saint: an unalterable figure that exists by his very believable human complexity, contradictions and earthy goodness.
The same applies with the character of Atticus Finch and the genuine depth of resentment, expressed by some, at the news of a previously written novel by Harper Lee, showing a less racially tolerant (and no less fictional) Atticus Finch: these readers somehow taking issue with what was Miss Harper Lee's absolute creative right with her characters: ironically proving how well she succeeded in making Atticus Finch's fictional existence so real to the reader, as to be untouchable.

Morsels of Hope

The last wireless of the village had been long ago confiscated;
But horrible news is perversely efficient: "The Nazis were coming south."
At the butcher,
a few remaining pieces of miserable beef... and much talk about
increased military traffic.
That night... the first of too many...
the four walls of the tiny kitchen took the appearance of a life-boat.
The family... had stopped giving illusory glances toward the cupboards.

The father, an avid reader, despite his limited formal education,
Had lined the walls with books, as some sort of insulation from the
outside world.
His precious history books:
History... the past... from which "to predict the future" he would say.

And so... sadness added itself to his fear for his family:
"Vandals at the door of the city": he murmured to his stupefied children,
With infernal visions... of mud covered barbarians
looting the eternal capital of the eternal empire...Rome.

His family.... Typical product of years of catechism...
had been touched first-hand by the glue of Jewish rituals
of neighbors, long ago gone into the surrounding hills.

That evening meal and the many others through the occupation,
In an un-verbalized acquiescence, took on the magic of a Last Supper.

Nightly ceremonials as intimate acts of resistance
In the name of a secular faith of solidarity.

Nights when the plates were practically empty
But the souls well fed.

And thus, that night...
The first at the entrance into the depth of human darkness;
The first... with some vestige of any illusion of hope:

For they knew… they all knew…
That they would make it…
As the mother, in a surrealistic moment of defiance,
Pulled out… like a holy relic… the last jar of confit.
—Her last preserve of duck confit, hidden in the back of the hutch—

Then, almost as an answer to the rhetorical question from the
Old aunt in her rocking chair:
"Alors… qu'est-ce qu'on devient maintenant?" **

… The mother, in the most natural tone replied:
"Je vais préparer votre plat favori." ***

There would be months of betrayals from friends and neighbors.
Months of heartbreaking devotion from others.

But there existed in this supper, and its dignified religiosity,
Gestures… containing an eternity.

Moments … when members would recall their place at the table;
When someone said: "Mangeons… on s'en sortira." ****

Reconstructed moments in the city of Plan de Cuque, France, November 1942

** *"So… what will become of us now?"*
*** *"I'm going to prepare your favorite dish."*
**** *"Let's eat… we'll make it."*

*The French writer, Vercors, describes a scene (Le silence de la mer [Désespoir est mort]
{The silence of the sea: Despair is death}) outside a military mess-hall in a defeated
France of 1940. The soldiers have lost the battle, the war and their honor. They are
early for supper and sit on the sidewalk, dejected, when reappear the hilarious "military"
parade of ducklings from the village. Their surprisingly healthy laughter leads one of
them to grab tightly the upper shoulder of his colleagues as he gets up and say loudly…
"Let's eat… we'll make it."*

Of Skin Tones and Other Non-Conforming Leanings

If only…
We could insert more of these iconic Hollywood moments,
in the mundane of living:
The disincarnated, off-camera voices…

Of a life-saver, heart surgeon,
The announcement from the pilot, after a white-knuckle landing,
The soothing voice of an E.M, T. on the side of the road,
Finally putting a face to the "nice kindergarten teacher,"
The gruff face attached to the calloused, helping hand for a fellow,
pregnant subway passager,

… All and any other forms
of the sheer… human, color and gender-blind… nobility of solidarity
In our otherwise metaphysically orphaned status.

… This other…
Defined by haphazard molecular changes in skin tonality and various
other leanings
While evolving and traveling north from mankind's African birthplace.

"On making his discovery, the astronomer had presented it to the International Astronomical Congress, in a great demonstration. But he was in Turkish costume, and so nobody would believe what he said.
Grown-ups are like that…."
[Le petit prince by Antoine de Saint Exupéry]

And the injustice suffered by Alan Turing for his sexual leaning despite his incalculable contribution during World War II.

Right of Shelter

The "Negro Travelers' Green Book" of the Jim Crow era, compared to the iconic nomadic traditions of the desert-traveler's right of shelter under a stranger's tent and his meager food.

Branding the other... as the eternal other.
That person at the door... as part of the trees.

No semblance of humanity,
In those tired bones.

A sweaty presence on the porch,
Around a missing image.

Like a perverted magic trick,
The passing of a magician's stick,
The waving of the circus entertainer's cloth:

The MAN... ripped suit case and scuffed shoes,
Having vanished in fumes of injustice.

Infernal alchemy, in a Sunday-school... white teacher's... white glance,
Fueled by minute layers of skin cells... spread as a malignancy by history.

The Negro Motorist Green Book *(at times styled* The Negro Motorist Green-Book *or titled* The Negro Travelers' Green Book*) was an annual guidebook for African-American road trippers, commonly referred to simply as the Green Book. It was originated and published by New York City mailman Victor Hugo Green from 1936 to 1966, during the era of Jim Crow laws, when open and often legally prescribed discrimination against non-whites was widespread. Although pervasive racial discrimination and black poverty limited car ownership, the emerging African-American middle class bought automobiles as soon as they could. In response, Green expanded the coverage in his book from the New York area to much of North America, also founding a travel agency.*

Yard Sale

At what point…
Before the yearly church donation,
Maybe in anticipation of a new dress for his wife,
Or a new roof for the shed…

Did he sit, at the solid oak desk, put on his reading glasses,
Stroked his hunting dog's head…

… Did he, take inventory of his slaves?
Calculated his needs and plans?
Ask for his spouse's advice?

And in a flourish of black ink, write in his leather-bound ledger:
"Strong middle-aged black woman, good cook."

And added: "With or without child."

Reflection on a comment on Black America and the banjo instrument (on N.P.R.) and the general inhumanity of the institution of slavery.

Since slaves represented a sort of currency, slave owners were known to sell some of their holdings for an influx of cash (not unlike cashing stocks or C.D.'s) and would, if necessary, have to break up families (see in particular the sale of slaves to help Georgetown University's finances).

La Cathédrale de Chartres

She had indeed been like the untouchable image of his catechism days:
The porcelain face of eternal youth, dressed in white and pale blue..

High up behind the side altar:
Away from common human hands and impure human thoughts.

He was now in front of the massive doors… made beyond human scale
From medieval trees long sacrificed for human pride.

This house in the name of divine motherhood
Superbly given the appearance of a floating quarry

By men trying to transgress the laws of physics
With these towers seemingly pointing into some invisible cosmic entrance.

All these thoughts and other intemporal images
Going through the humble mind of the humble pilgrim,

As he feels the hardness of the granite stairs turning to gentleness
—Maybe, as a symbol of the worth of his presence—

Reflection upon teaching for years about the iconic importance of the cathedral de Chartres and then finally standing at the base its magnificent bell towers, only to realize that I am standing in dog feces.

Eden... Revisited

It should have been a denatured way to see each other:
The architectural polished marble and steel frigidity
Of a first-rate symposium, in first-rate site.

In lieu of the rustic intimacy of a "maid's quarters" in Montmartre.

—A properly dignified birthplace for the prose of political position papers—

Enough disincarnated intellectual activity
To keep the embers of their elementary instincts otherwise occupied,
in their assigned lecture halls.

Still...
Unrepentant passionate lovers... and now, outwardly,
Each other's best friend:
With remnants of hot flashes at the mere sound of her first name,
During the opening assembly.

Oh... some mundane concerns remained:
About the possibility of extra gray hair for him...
Or a cream-resistant wrinkle, near her lips.

Possibly the lack of topics for small talk:
The continuing hopes and expectations of advancement
and publication for both:
Those banalities... that pass for living.

Not even the fear of decrepitude...
Which had been the favorite theme of some of his early writings.

Not one... of these very normal human concerns... did he feel!

He DID fear... the possibility of discerning ambivalence in their
respective glances:
The deadening effects of the eternity of their separation.

The fear, of possibly seeing only a two-dimensional image:
Where had existed the rich layers of flesh against living flesh.

Yet...
To his heart-stopping amazement
—Not unlike a drug induced hallucination—

... He felt a weightlessness of the soul.

A *divine dispensation* rained upon them... a quasi-reformed Genesis:
They were exceptionally given the right of return to the uncomplicated
innocence of Paradise.

Thus... tasting once more,
Their first cup of coffee...
And the absence of time... thereafter.

Two ex-lovers (fellow academics), at a professional symposium.

Blue Metallic Swans

Homage to Salvador Dali

Having left
The luxuriant world of flowers outside his wide-open bedroom windows.
Exotic birds from the north,
Spending warm winter-days in the warm vapors from eucalyptus.

Nature would brush itself in a pointillism of colors,
Made of the deepest red dots from the cannac flowers in the yard
And the blackish green of the mulberry trees.

Nervous flight of huge, black red-dotted butterflies
And the incessant Greek-chorus background of cicadas.

It was as though the mind had maliciously chosen
To introduce an antithetical universe.

A sort of anti-matter, away from the organic:
Tactile gentleness and soft impressionism.

In this infernal labyrinth of infectious delirium,
Invaded by two-dimensional metallic profiles of blue swans,
Rocking endlessly back and forth
On decoupage cut-outs of silly looking waves.

And then…
The hopelessness of endless torture of an endless repeated spectacle…

Until… until… a scream from space…
And the awareness of strong arms behind the shoulders.

The familiarity of a father's squinting eyes.
And being brought back to the unquestioned reality of love.

Memories of visions while coming out of delirium-induced encephalic fevers in the Maghreb.

Anonymous Happiness

Only fake jewel incrustations on the thimble.
Yellowish gold-imitation paint for hardware.
'Secret' compartments on the side panels for tiny accessories.
An assortment of cheap colored threads neatly stacked:

… A Thousand and one nights' splendor…

For a nine-year-old, on the gray cobble-stones of a small garrison city,
Of a defeated nation… on a defeated continent.

She would pass by this treasure in the shop window,
Giving it one last glance on the way to school.

The adults in her life never did realize,
That in the middle of the hellish madness of war and atrocities
—On the third shelf, next to the plastic dolls—
Existed this glorious symbol to earthly happiness and everlasting hope.

Little French girl during world war two, at the height of the German occupation, gets her turn to tell the class about her Christmas gifts and says that she had received a sewing kit: She had, in reality, received not a single thing.

She tells a family gathering, decades later, that she had felt ashamed, since all the other students had received at least one gift.

Glorification of Emotional Pain

Having last seen him… last man standing,
Proudly intact, with a battle field covered with bleeding broken hearts:

He had put his three Greek letters on the map:
And his week-end conquests in the rumor mill.

A fabricator of artificial integrity. Master of genuine fakery.
Unfailingly attractive to the opposite sex;
And worthy of reluctant admiration from the rest of the fourth floor.

A perfect enigma to any of us: self-respecting existentialists:
This man had an unexplainable multitude of consciences.

No philosophical direction; but rather an uncanny eye
For the still youthful susceptibility behind the next luscious lips in his class.

There was a surprising good natured simplicity in publicizing his conquests
A jaded recalling of the emotional carnage.
The totality of these self-assured intimacies
Created a pointillism of stains.

Nothing would ever dare stand between his roving fingers and the next impulse
He would be destined for ultimate envy and success in life and living.

———————————————

A chance meeting, years later, painted a surreal carnal desert of body parts
Separated from their respective soul.
His victims… like Goya studies, had been properly slain.

And in a Scotch induced confession,
In the lobby of a third-class hotel of a third-class city,
From all the amazing beauty that he had embraced,
He admitted under his alcoholic breath…
"remembering not the beauty… but the tears, in all their eyes."

Chance re-encounter with an ex-dormitory classmate: a university campus "legend with women."

Charlie Hebdo

The absolute sinful terror.
Complete moral disintegration.
Sexual frenzy taking over decision-making in the free-wheeling editorials.

No divine direction.
No pronouncement from the God-fearing authorities.
No stern commandments and no laws to control the lowest animal instincts
from rising to the front of the first page.

This was a place from which… at any time…
From anyone of a group of bright lunatics,

Could and would emanate drawings full of deviant behavior
and an absence of restraint.
All painstakingly presented with surgical pen and ink illustrations.

What better example, therefore…
Of the splendid, civilized zest for tolerance…

Than the contrasting inner beauty of the scatological drawings,
Left hurriedly abandoned under the drawing tables:

As the blood of the dying artist
Creates impressionistic red clouds over the figure… of a nun…
On a moped…
Habit flying over her shapely thighs!

"Laughter and sex scare the oppressive leaders and religions:"
Comments from the new editor of Charlie Hebdo *after the Paris attacks.*

"Les vignes sont comme la vie… et la vie c'est le risque." **

She had the wisdom that years impose on the soul:
Two grown children and hours of childhood fevers.

Living knows how to impress us with the resilience of life.

Bud killing frost…
Akin to some malediction from the god living in nearby medieval church:
Equating the heartbreak of raising children
To the one of making wine.

———————————————————————

And yet… in early spring, under a single drop of dew,
From a shy sliver of green, on the side of the twisted wood,
Like the discernable smile on the child's lips upon a fever's break,

The mother knows… she recognizes the signs,
Of a natural law akin to a quasi-human trait,

Found in these tough, emaciated vines:
Rewarding her care and feasting their survival
with vermilion splendor.

** *"Grapevines are like life… and life is risk."*

Near Château-Neuf-du-Pape, late spring: asked about the uncertainties of running a vineyard, the owner looks away from the camera and after enumerating all the times when the weather almost destroyed her vines, she exhales as though she had been holding her breath and says: "Les vignes sont comme la vie… et la vie… c'est le risque."

The Death of the Author

Homage to Roland Barthes

Could it be that the author died on an early autumn night?
Not on the slippery leaves of a rural New England road.
But at his writing desk.

The man, had been overwhelmed with images and perfumed scents.
And had taken his place in a quasi-medieval ritual;
The alchemy of recreating and preserving the past.

In this fable, the author leaves his human body,
To better examine his multiple cross-reflections on facing mirrors.
Letting streams of consciousness take the reins,
Thus, offering his eventual reader the means to, in turn, relive moments.

Precious moments that have enchanted humanity.
These moments like the magic of a slow dance:
Trembling fingers on lacy black silk and warm bare skin.

Not really unlike the passion of prehistoric creativity,
Of a caveman, his muddy fingers on the wet stone of a grotto,
Fashioning figures that would transcend the now.

In both of these intemporal acts, exist…
A recognition… an awareness… of Time and its laws.

When the artist symbolically steps aside…dies… leaving the text behind
Letting his art survive without his bodily weight.

———————————————————

Let's rejoice along with our prehistoric ancestor
As we appreciate our presences, at arm's length in front of the
flatness of the drawing,
As less important than the illusion created by the picture.

This must have been the first flirting with sacrificing artistically of oneself:
Somehow sprinkling pieces of thoughts,
In a duality of author and reader.

Art and the very act of creativity,
As an escape-door to other dimensions.
Like a one-way ticket out of the soporific happiness of Paradise

Mankind… in its own created world,
Able to assume the role of the gods:
With rules to be challenged at will and in all possible ways.

The Great Marquis de Sade, having made
himself the misunderstood instrument
Of this heavy responsibility of artistic freedom.

All this past and culture that the poet embodies:
Bringing him to his desk… on that night,
To capture once more evaporated moments of her presence in his arms.

Him… the rumored saintly man…
Creating crimson reality from the lives around the sedate cafeteria table.
Often using the innocent third person to cover over the first.
Acting as accidental voyeur.
Choosing arbitrarily degrees of distance and liberty
With the text.

A liberal view of Roland Barthes' seminal work La mort de l'auteur.

In his story Sarrasine, Balzac, speaking of a castrato disguised as a woman, writes this sentence: "It was Woman, with her sudden fears, her irrational whims, her instinctive fears, her unprovoked bravado, her daring and her delicious delicacy of feeling." Who is speaking in this way? Is it the story's hero, concerned to ignore the castrato concealed beneath the woman? Is it the man Balzac, endowed by his personal experience with a philosophy of Woman? Is it the author Balzac, professing certain "literary" ideas of femininity? Is it universal wisdom? or romantic psychology? It will always be impossible to know, for the good reason that all writing is itself this special voice, consisting of several indiscernible voices, and that literature is precisely the invention of this voice, to which we cannot assign a specific origin: literature is that neuter, that composite, that oblique into which every subject escapes, the trap where all identity is lost, beginning with the very identity of the body that writes. (The Death of the Author {Roland Barthes})

Canaries in the Coal Mines

He scanned the tableau-vivant of youth,
In staid deep-veined walnut surroundings.

Ivy-covered, granite-block buildings,
In this New England cocoon incubator.

A pool for future humanistic skeptics…
Tadpoles critics of accepted truths, from any adults above their age.

All these young minds sent on expensive parental-funded quests:
To inevitably challenge their parents' very authority.

This next generation, had been handed mini hammers
With which to chip at the cement of traditions… from anyone…
regarding anything.

The venerable old professor…
Had turned his back… Faced the black board…
And was clumsily searching for a bigger piece of white chalk.

He resembled an actor starting his favorite soliloquy:
Right arm stretching at forty five degree;
Left… in a perfect opposite counter balance.

He had begun the grossly enlarged convex curve of the letter "D"…
An "encore" of his favorite lecture was about to begin:

The birth of Cartesian skepticism… was going to explode on the board.
He stopped…
As though struck by his anticipated second heart attack.

He was, in reality, silently contemplating to himself:
"What could be…
A singly symbolic icon of personal experience…
What can I spread…
Over this field of fertile soil… as seeds of defiance?
What words…
Would wrench this Monday morning assembly out of its torpor?

What could possibly...
Leave them with a vivid image in their eyes?
What viscerally intimate face...
In their lives, could be linked to an organic solution... a revolution?"

And thus, it came to be...
That, from this quasi reclusive... painfully private... brilliant... cold and
analytical mind...
—apparently more in his world among graphed equations—

Was uttered... to a mesmerized and, for once, non-jaded amphitheater...
A confessional voice:
Memories of his mother... and other mother-figures...

... Deeply personal visions of Bronx tenement kitchen-scenes.
Mother's grueling hours as house-cleaner. Abuse-filled subway rides.
Drunken insults from uncles and anonymous disrespect from passing-cars.

All of this gut-wrenching lyricism,
Coming from this ossified academic...

From the protection of a tiny wooden table...
With a sad grin of exhausted satisfaction.

*From an exasperated government professor (circa 1950's): "You know what... we are
wasting our time, in academia, writing formal papers on the most reliable indicators for
good governance of societies... its best indicator is the level of freedom and respect of its
feminine population."*

Simply… a Convenient Place in Which to Die

Albert Camus died in a car accident, January 4th, 1960 at the age of 46

In Bourgogne, near the City of Sens,
In the section of Le Grand Fossard of the little town of Villeblevin,

Around the first decades of peace,
After World War II in France,

A road crew
Must have been assigned to geometrically plant
Straight rows of future majestic trees,
Lovingly aligned
Toward some imaginary infinite.

Thirty years later,
A winter-day's honor-guard of leafless trunks,
Still neatly arranged and now amazingly strong,

Guided the writer,
Into a continuation of nothingness begun at his birth:

And not much different than the moments before his death,
When mindlessly puffing on an ever-present cigarette.

And so,
This beautiful mind was proven splendidly correct,
By dying in this quaint wine region,
On his way to an anticipated intimate meal;

Against this tree, that remained
Completely oblivious as to its part in this human tragedy.

Flâner dans Paris **

Hommage to Charles Baudelaire's Le Spleen de Paris

He had been looking for a short cut to the Seine:
Take a right at the bouquinistes
And then…
It was as though all his senses had been…
uncontrollably possessed… turned on.
As though he was being violated… vulnerably undressed:

The wetness of the walls acquired a silverish patina.
The organic smells of decay of the historic sewers,
Created a welcoming Film Noir envelope.

He could swear… detecting quasi-musical rhythmic moans,
From behind the swaying curtains above.

He knew… he viscerally knew
That there was nothing to fear from all of this:
That the darkness was nuptial. **

That this tragic street corner, was atoning
For the blood spilled by the Gestapo and revolutionaries.

It contained the privileged aura of some places on earth:
Places, made of similar corners, in all the vastness of galaxies.

Places of miraculous gravitational attraction
That produce life and living… in an otherwise disinterested and sterile universe.

This street… and these stones…
A laboratory of sources for the rich primordial soup
Of sentient existence in the vastness of things
And the reason for his presence in this city…

… Having repeated, earlier in her arms, his favorite Credo:
"You know you are happy when it would feel right to die."

He had unconsciously brought his left hand to his nostrils:
A rich… acrid mixture…
Of sweetness, time, images, ethics and responsibilities
… exploded in his soul.

It felt to him, as though Nature
Would not allow such truths to be hidden.

As though…
Whole worlds of stars, were dancing on his index:
Worlds full of vanished commandments, oaths and constraints.

Layers of his structured life
Had seemingly been ripped off, in bloody displays,
At his trembling feet, on the Gothic cobblestones.

His youthful Catechism had told him about these sacrilegious hours.
Times…
When, before his expulsion, the beautiful Lucifer,
from the right hand-side of God,
Had represented those perilous truths and beauty.

Big Bang remnants of which, he had just seen,
In her flesh, presence, glance, voice and pregnant silence.

She had redefined Humanity and its very downfall,
Through her swoons.

Destroying an academic career and wisdom worth of books,
By simply acquiescing in whispers of unspoken desire.

She had been… in that room… on that bed…
All that should be… just… in a just universe:

That is….
A last vestige of conscience… before its opposite.

Strolling through Paris (very late at night)
*** Victor Hugo: "Booz endormi" ["Boaz asleep"]*

Meursault in Love

A nihilist... in love

Typical disorder, of typical university dormitory room:
Surroundings made of the ferment of humanistic thought of lecture halls.

Temptations of carefree hedonism and experimentation,
In the image of this multi-function bed:
Sleep. Dining. Studying.
With interspaced reconstructions—on a blander scale—
Of moments of *Philosophy in the bedroom*

Future converts to absurdism and nihilism:
Marquis De Sade. Nietzsche. Camus.
Thanks to these mermaid calls from the exotic. The contradictory.

The tantalizingly destructive of good mannered Catechism:
Plunging into the darkish-abyss corners of *Thought and Thinking*.

And then, the inevitable, Meursault... in love.
In love in a nihilistic world.
On this bed, looking into hazel-eyed tomorrows.

Yes! Guilty, of glorifying moments, lyricism, feelings.
This would-be character of The Stranger:
Here, on this bed, expressing strange thoughts.

Strange passion, expressed by words seemingly dying
at the rate of their expression.

Their presence on this bed:
In the absolute conviction of the immortality of the moment ...
Flying in the face of the anti-apotheosis, experienced years earlier,

Sitting, at the end of a father's death bed:
And now, trying to reconcile: Things. Emotions. People.
And their opposite.

Alcohol, Fornication, Art and Other Things

A burden of mankind… imposed on itself, wanting to know:
To know about the box… that box in which we seem to exist.

Maybe God's Big Bang remnants of his damning voice
to the sinning couple:
Scurrying out of the Garden of Genesis.

A loss of intellectual innocence…
possibly engendering an irresistible drive
For confirmation of some ancestry:
Having refused the orphan status of being the
result of simple stellar dust.

Mankind, unlike rutting chimpanzees, not satisfied
Living on the pastel green at their feet:
Having looked up between frolics... having wondered.

Conceiving the infinity of numbers
A metaphor started for numbering the steps to the end of the village,
The birth of a child or the death of a mother.

We are still waiting for the identity of the code-writer,
Using some our favorite hedonistic pastimes
As descendants of that infamous Garden,

Such as alcohol, fornication, art and other things:
Waiting for that presence behind the curtain to be either,
Real, or this self-imposed cosmic-waste of time.

"Infinity… This is how the concept of God should be explained…," seating in a bull-session of an over-heated university dormitory room. Referring to calculus class topic of dividing something by zero or the infinite approach of the asymptotic-line of an equation.

Of Marie Antoinette and Madame Bovary

Ritualistically stifled… Historically entrapped.
Corsets laced into the reddened flesh:
Metaphors for the end of frolics in flowered gardens.

Perky personality, exuberance of youth…
Sternly frowned into noble submission.

The fatal experience begun in the charade of quasi-pedophilial nuptials;
And the starvation of adult happiness.

Very human and very normal blooming
Of sensual and hedonistic appetites:

Satisfied by rumored sampling of ladies in waiting
And the sweetness of Parisian confiseries.

The green sprouts of wild grass… properly covered over
In gilded aristocratic splendors:
Themselves, the image of the artificial order of nobility.

Like an espalier tree-grove, unnatural leanings,
Mercilessly imposed: upon people and nature.

Any conceivable remnants of teenage whispered phantasms uprooted:
She would conform… and be a queen… even if fatal.

Later… in a created world of created fiction,
Appearing in the cold wording style from an overheated soul,
From a writer… Having lost his own identity,
In the ultimate Faustian bargain of created reality:

Proudly confessing:
"Madame Bovary, c'est moi."

A woman,
With ingrained flowing girlish reveries of waltzes in twirling silk,
Fed by fantasies and illusions built by dreams of romantic love,
On the hardwood reality of a dull dance floor, in the arms of a dull husband.

And so, cry for these pure breeds,
Especially made for the rarest substance of the perfumed scent:
That of extravagant freedom, edgy personal excitement and experimentation.

Life and society
Having proclaimed that the mold would mold them.
The Arbitrary would write the rules.

It seems, that vaporous sensuality had descended into these women,
From their unfulfilled ancestry.

All of these nights of subdued sighs into their pillow.
All of the erotic dreams,
Next to the dull flesh imposed on them.

All the cold breath, of proper womanly conduct,
Cooling the willing, waiting sweaty flesh.

All this energy, wanting to throw wide open the wood-shutters!
And allow their bodies the joys of the next hours.

All of this… and none of it…
Reality having become their destiny,

In their escape through the edge of a metal wedge and a bitter chemical taste.

Liberal reflection upon these women (historical in one case and mostly fictional in the other), seemingly doomed by their gender, perceived temperamental unsuitability… and their times.

Love... Un-verbalized: *A fable*

Now navigating the darkish waters
Of the uncharted and unchartable.

A microcosm filled with the voids of past, present and future.
As well as, absolutes that only mankind's creation of wars can accomplish.

Carrying in their respective flight,
Atomized pieces of their identity as socialized animals:
Along with anguished thoughts of having lost everything. **

Self-guided relationship:
With merely their conscience as a North Star.

It was not what was said to the other, or how well,
During these eight weeks.

It was rather... the discerned hints, the human indicators,
Overlooked in the course of normal times,

Hours in a neo-Gothic ruin
In this decrepit basement, once the pride of a cultured bishop.

Just enough natural light
Allowing facial decryption and adding an ironic nuptial encouragement to
the shadows.

It is when the subtleties of emotions cannot be properly articulated
That the unarticulated is primordial

Eloquent only in their respective tongue
They became fluent in the other's voice:

Halting sadness,
Flowing syllables of pre-war joys.

The pathetic tonality of past hopes and lives
Miraculously cross-interpreted.

Un-verbalized courtesies:
Offering a wood-box for a seat and a moldy cheese.

The instinctive wiping of their tears
At the sight of wrinkled photographs

––––––––––––––––––––

A confessional hush seemed to have existed
Between them, over these hours.

It was, as though, they had been afraid of being overheard
By walls that had lost their consecrated integrity.

In wartime... Reality...
Does not suffer well vaporous philosophy,

During those times, symbolic pieces of bread and some wine,
remain in that state,
Without acquiring the redemptive power of a simple human embrace...

Shot down over the eastern front of World War II Europe, a surviving German pilot (a reluctant convert to the Nazi party), comes across an escaped Jewish woman; in a wasteland of destroyed and deserted villages. A setting potentially deadly for either, from all sides. Neither speaks the other's language.

** "La culture, c'est ce qui reste chez l'homme quand il a tout oublié"
"Culture is what is left in man when he has forgotten everything."
Nota bene: There are several versions and attributed forms of this quote. (possibly Édouard Erriot)

The Painter Who Painted With His Eyes...

In homage to Turner and Courbet.

He had walked near the floor-to-ceiling window:
Pivotal hour in a city...
When late-night revelers cross path with cafés setting up.

As though, by decree,
A portion of society must always be awake,
In order, not to let sleep take over living:
Like the prehistoric "keeper of the fire."

Life and loving, had to continue unabated.
Separating out, ennui and the mundane.
Taxis and trains. Conferences and symposia,

A dizzying existentialist nausea invaded his thoughts.
His body seemed to impulsively twist back towards the bed.

The display on it, anchored his soul once again:
In the penumbra, made of moonlight and morning sun,
He could discern wavelets made of sheets and flesh.

A canvas of creamy-white cotton and pinkish, lustful incarnation.
Quasi-tropical slumber and perfumes.
Femininity of the curves.
Guiltless innocence of tabernacle offerings.
Full of the understated internal volcanic heat.
Languorous angle of the right arm.
Slight opening of the thighs,
Leading to various nuances of darkness.

He could not breathe:
From fear of losing the moment...
The noiseless-street now paying its respect.

He thought about his old art professor:
The one with the smile of a self-assured teen-ager,
The one constantly walking back and forth in front of his slides:

Creating surrealist imagery
Of pliable nudity over his enormous body.

And his commandment:
"Paint with your eyes… ˙
Some moments in life are too precious to be touched by paint or chisel."

Standing in awe, next to the bed, he added in a whisper:
"Indeed… not unlike the stylet for the Tora…
If only we could paint with our eyes.!"

Paris, sixième arrondissement hôtel.

Birth of a Muse

Roissy-Charles de Gaulle airport, international departures:
He: "I have been made different by you..."

Intimate whispered dialog...
Somehow feeling irrationally afraid
That the gods would hear him confess the rich complexity
of moments with her.

Like these rituals in Provence, when the villagers eat omelets,
Made with slices of rich truffles,
While covering the dish and their heads under a cloth:
So, as to not cause the jealous envy of the gods:

Happiness... has always been a rare commodity... Even for those gods.
And artists, through human passion itself, have earned their indulgence:
Allowing mere mortals, the divine privilege of, once more, tasting last night.

Happiness resurrected from the very soul of the artist,
As he makes possible, through his art, the transference of our own moments:
Through a chiaroscuro, that depicts contradictions of soul;
A watery sunrise, that gives solidity to the nuances of emotions;
A soliloquy, seemingly stating, center stage, murmurs from our heart.

Precious moments from yesterday,
Inspired into a mosaic ... stone by marble stone.

And, unlike the scientist, bound by the rational...
The artist... now alone in front of his cooling coffee,
Dares to contradict the order of things...
that time is a cosmic... forward... one-way street.

Deluded, but valiant,
The artist blows on the embers of the past embodied by an invisible presence
Sitting... once more... across from him.

Had she not left for another place, another life, there would not have existed this rationally,
unbridgeable void that artists have used as a source of created past reality.

Fictional Existence

Reflection on the depth of resentment reported by some at the news of a previously written (and subsequently released) novel by Harper Lee, showing a less racially tolerant Atticus Finch. Somehow reacting as though taking issue with Miss Harper Lee's absolute creative freedom and ironically proving how well she had succeeded in making Atticus Finch's exemplary 'fictional existence' so real, likeable and vital to the reader. There is no better example of the power of fiction that the repulsive concept of a bigoted, less perfect Atticus Finch or a socio-pathological Jean Valjean, had their authors willed it: and in Harper Lee's case, she had.

Instructional initiation of our universe to fiction:
A process, known as the roulette-wheel of a 'book assignment'.

The fruit of curricula from endless meetings
or from the teacher's personal taste.
Rite of passage of high school English class project:
A reluctant interference with teen-age week-end plans.

Surprisingly, at times, leading to the quiet of late-night reading
—under warmth of a bedspread—
—maybe "a dark and windy night... —"

And then... this magic pull of words:
Images... emotions... fever from the paragraphs.

Maybe a recurring obsession with the heroine's eyes
And a similarity with those of a real girl in algebra class?

What is this alchemic cross-fertilization
Of pieces of one reality invading another?

Is this when we were introduced
To the endless existence of multiple universes?

Is this invented world of fiction mankind's attempt
At distraction for living in this corner of our galaxy?

A grandiose, generous awareness.
A collective experience.
A solidarity in human emotions... in its innumerable archetypes.

A quasi-divine power, given to the mind of the artist
And his free-hand at phantasms of characters and situations

The artist able to create his own worlds of gods and crystalline goodness
Or of the angels like Lucifer, beautiful and rebellious.

Thoughts on being introduced to the existence of Jean Valjean, early in French schools: This persona, in his complexity, contradictions and goodness, a creation from the mind of Victor Hugo, could not be anything short of a secular saint to me. An un-alterable figure as solid as the furniture in my room.

Exhilaration of Absolute Freedom

Reflecting on reports that some of the slaves transported to the American continent chose to jump into the ocean.

This must have been, for some the exhilaration of absolute freedom:
That bird-like flight into the saltiness of ocean spray.

Maybe, one last glance into the oppressor's eyes:
With frozen white smirk** towards him,

One last noble statement… a warning of the unstoppable
drive for rebellion.
The Sisyphean dignity of resistance,
Still burning in the heart of the miserable cargo in the hold.

Any justice, that means anything, must have been encapsulated
In the useless obscenities in the rage of the captain:

Insulted… in his belief of the omnipotent righteousness
Of one man's mastery over another,

As he detects, dumfounded, one last time,
Before it disappears in the green ocean…

A further example of humanity's rumored joyful beatitude,
As it faces its tragedies.

** *It is said that some were smiling on the way down to their death*

Saint Malo

Blind man with his guide-dog on empty beach of Saint Malo,** during the quiet stillness of an early September. The man's companion gently unleashes the animal who looks up in confusion and then starts to pace in circles. She, again shoos it gently away... pointing at the beach. The dog seems to finally understand, running like mad towards the water, to promptly run back. She extends her arm again and the dog now runs with abandonment in large circles on the beach, playfully skimming the wavelets. All the while, the man stands almost motionless, his arms dangling by his side... there is a hint of puzzled smile on his lips...

Privileged voyeuristic moment:
A feeling of my intrusion into the intimacy of another's personal emotions.

And yet, I choose to believe that this man is feeling
A rare awareness of limitless expanse,
Rather than the familiar echoes of nearby walls.

The presence of visual void, translated through a synesthesia of sounds:
Creating the impression of free movement through repetitive
Receding and approaching joyful barking.

The faithful beast, innocently breaking his master's heart
By translating without pity the sensuality of freedom of sight,
Through the lyricism of making him hear... what sight must be.

And then... That night, on his blanket, at the foot of the bed,
This animal dreams, once more, of running
Towards where the water meets the sand.

** Saint Malo, in Normandie, France, is known for its powerful tides: The ocean can pull back hundreds of yards.

Hermaphrodite World

*How would societies and civilizations have evolved, if humans had been born with both
genders in each of us?*

Teenage dances, with an air of monastery calm…
No need for girls and boys leaning on opposite walls,
Feverishly eyeing "that other weird sex!"

One o'clock in the morning…
Undergraduate university men's dormitories, quietly studying for exams:
Not getting ready for a 'panty-raid.'

While co-eds, sitting cross-legged in their pajamas,
review for their mid-terms:
Foregoing, to openly grade the various masculinity of their last dates.

Earlier on the time-scale, vandals entering Rome…
Simply taking the expensive tableware and not harming a hair
on the temple vestals:
Their porcelain bodies, under translucent garments, causing no interest.

Invading armies of the past… looking for local women,
Simply to make them cook a good meal.

Office romances…
Would be about anything but sexual attraction… a sexy BMW maybe.

In the words of Woody Allen…
Sex, would indeed be like self-gratification with your
Best friend, since it would be you.

Aggression, dominance and possession…
Would have had, as their source, the strength of ideas
And not the size of a prehistoric club.

A Foretaste of America

Earliest remembrance of the taste of Coca Cola in Morocco (circa 1950's)

Solidity of noontime North African heat:
It followed you into the miniscule grocery store.

There... in the corner, to the right, a bright-red addition to the store.
A quasi-treasure... this metallic ice box:
Stocked with strangely shaped bottles.
Inside, a suspiciously darkish liquid,
More like my father's dark Martinique rum.

Foregoing, this time, the locally made Orangina. **

It was, at first, the smoky sweetness of the invading burst of bubbles.
A gentle, scratching feeling on the back of the throat,
Added to the rarity of refrigerated coldness.

But it was the foreign sweetness...
The unknown sensual sweetness enveloping the tongue.
A vague awareness that the body
Was in the presence of something that had been lacking all this time.

Ah! To recreate... to relive this privileged moment...
That of the first time in one's life.

To relive the sorcery of rich revelations that surprise one's body
When introduced to the new.

The whole moment re-enacted over the years
By the properly staged... heat... cold... and smell on my lips.

Memories of drinking from this strange looking bottle for the first time, in a grocery store that barely had electricity. The owner pulled out a cold bottle from a red metal box. Its sweet perfume tickled my nostrils and the effervescence of the bubbles created a confusion of the senses: a synesthesia that recreates, when least expected in the summer heat of New England, this Proustian moment... in my youth... in Morocco when America first touched me.

*** There was an Orangina manufacturing plant in the city of Kenitra (formerly Port-Lyautey), Morocco.*

Emotional Quotient

Homage to the "Kiss," by Auguste Rodin

Foundation of their whole world:
Religious canonic icon… there… at the beginning,
In an otherwise secular, hedonistic dimension.

Eternally there… an impeachable measure of
Untouchable white marble reference.

Polar star… in the otherwise darkness of nights,
guiding him, guiding them,
Back to the micro-second before their closing eyelids:
Holding the heading toward precious lips.

And then… explosive contact of a Genesis.
After eons of galactic wanderings in stellar clouds:
Leading to this beachhead of anti-void.

It could have be,en in the coldness of a science laboratory,
Akin to the parallel lines on a metal rod, a meter long, **
In the stabilized temperature of mankind feeble attempt to counteract time.

But this… this kiss…
Untouchable, in its white marble reference.
This kiss could not die… or they would.

Until… until his recollection of her:
After a chance meeting, years later, in the leftovers
In their favorite coffee shop.

Of the kiss… their kiss…
Untouchable white marble reference:

And her insistence, on now… *non-existent details*
And the unfathomable sadness of his drive home.

Trepidation, by the poet, upon reading the recurring, modern scientific evidence of the chemically-based process in our [very organic] organ—the brain—that involves the memory process. In this case of "a kiss"["the kiss"] as the subject of poetic lyricism. This evidence seems to imply a less than reliable human recollection of our past actions. Indications seem to imply that our very act or acts of remembering or trying to remember, are 'playing over' [not unlike a tape] the very details of memory and probably changing some of its details: A reflection that has driven poetry and poets.

** Official reference to the length of the meter as a specific fraction of the length of the arc of a latitude of the globe.

A Child's World

Protective cocoon of images
Forming a world in shades of simple pastels.

Those moments of a child's morning, made up of repeated happy endings.
Images of bubbling innocence,
Found in green open spaces of freedom of movement
And the friendship of objects.

A microcosm of those unsullied mornings
Made for the still unburdened souls of newborns.

Satisfying warm sheen of softness to the touch.
Seemingly bottomless peace of the inviting glance
And graceful elegance of a fawn.

Fluid form… creating, in the lyricism of this animal's movement,
A metaphor for the ephemeral qualities of youth:
Fated to be lost in the rites of adulthood.

Gazing at the motif of a child's bedroom wallpaper

Of Men and Butterflies

Nature does things properly, unapologetically
And very particularly... amorally.

He had walked into a perfect testing site,
A laboratory of sorts:
The end-game of Darwinism and perpetuation of genes.

A place and time
With no space and time
For the illusion of the delusions of Love:

The Harlequin paper-pulp version of Love.

For he had walked into the pollen covered world of waiting flowers,
With his over-sized eyes for only the next attractive flamboyance.

He would ignore all others and their waiting pistils,
For this one above all others:

The elated-elected one of his heart
With a future of a broken heart.

Having in a quick flap of his wings,
Found his new-found attraction
Of yet... a newer colorful pistil.

"Natasha's dress had a tendency to change colors in his memory. Sometimes she was 'wrapped in a dove-white dress accenting her perfect figure, which made her as arresting as Lana Turner in The Postman Always Rings Twice.*' Other times she was wearing 'all red.' Dad had brought a date, a Miss Lucy Marie Miller of Ithaca who was a new Associate Professor in Columbia's English Department. Dad could never remember what color she was wearing. He didn't even remember seeing Lucy, or saying good-bye to her, after their brief discussion about King Taa II's hip's remarkable state of preservation, because, moments later, he spotted the pale blond, aristocratically nosed Natasha Bridges standing in front of the knee and lower thigh of Ahmosis IV, chatting absentmindedly with her date, Nelson L. Aimes of the San Francisco Aimeses."*
[Otis Library Exquisite Writing Project, Ledyard, Connecticut]

Provençal Heat

Outside of Mons... Provençal noontime silent scene, in hilltop village of whitewash stone houses: the dry heat, the brightness of the sum, the dark-blue sky... and at the top of a curving stone staircase, to roof overlook... a deep-red shutter.

Mediterranean sharp solar delineation,
Admits a crystalline dryness of severe clair-obscur.

Majesty of whitewash solidity of cement steps,
Looking into the coolness of a cubist azure.

Dividing the canvas with disciplined
Spaces of surface textures.

All the while, this deceptively shy presence,
With a flavor of Proustian impressionism,*
Of a temptingly-opened red shutter,

Beaconing our gaze by its sanguine contrast...
Within the sternness of various earth tone shadings.

Treasures of early afternoon hedonistic slumber.
Full of the hot breath from the shores of the Classical world.

* *Reference to Marcel Proust's "pan de mur jaune" [section of yellow wall] in Vermeer's "View of Delft."*

"...That Was Before Gender Descended for Most of Us..." **

Little children, in school play-grounds:
Like so many stem-cells... self-contained entities.

Full of all possibilities.
Still animated with the potential of their respective potentials.

Little children, with the natural neutrality of their glance upon the world:
Presumed equanimity of self-worth or direction.

Beginnings full of self-discovery:
Subjecting themselves to curious self-examination:

"What to make... of this peculiar and apparently quaint piping,
With no particular origin... purpose... meaning... or prejudices?"

And then, the rites of passage: assimilation of that
Little girl into the maze of rituals.

The invariable frustrations of religious and secular laws.
The endgame for her various body parts.
The reconciling... by her and the Other...
Of the maternal signifier and the sensual signified.

That little girl learning, after some time, the lesson
That she had more freedom of action with her cotton doll
Then any future child she could ever have.

Encapsulation, in an ex-playboy bunny,
Of sexual freedom from sexual identity.

Little girl, now looking directly into her Teddy bear's plastic eyes...
Fathoming the integrity of her own soul.

** *Liberal reflection on Gloria Steinem's N.P.R., interview with Terry Gross: "Remember when you were 9 or 10 and you were this independent little girl climbing trees and saying, 'I know what I want, I know what I think?'" she says. "That was before gender descended for most of us."*

And God Created Adultery...

Speculating on God's reflection upon his creation of the couple in the Garden of Eden.

It could have been...
An unknowable happiness,
In a dumb and deaf world.

A world of sleepy stagnation,
In the still waters of endless repetition:

There would, simply, have been... No drama.

Families in pools of non-turbulence.
Couples in lasting harmony.
Races and religion not measuring their differences:
Eviscerating angst filled soliloquies.

Literature, indeed, about... "much to do about nothing."
Oedipus well-adjusted and Hamlet self-assured

Whole swath of unwritten folios.

Silenced operatic tears unheard:
Carmen perky... but well-behaved.
Jean Valjean, as a teenager, introduced to a wise bishop.

Human envies and appetites relegated
To quaint palpitations of imperceptible fever.

Locksmiths and divorce lawyers, like unused organs,
No more than withered appendages.

The exquisite or heart wrenching extremes of human emotions,
Just mere conceptual speculations:
Like multi-dimensional time and space spectrum.

Thus, like an adventurous and inventive chef,
The Eternal... changed eternity...
By adding a pinch of adultery and chaos to the recipe:

Letting the pot come to temperature and entertain audiences ever since.

Cosmologists speculate that "waves" of imperfections in the evolution and expansion of the universe made it more possible for the presence of exceptional or improbable changes that seem to have produced sentient life: in an otherwise uneventful dead one.

The Fragility of Happy Endings

Reflections on how some social prejudices have played into life and death issues. **

Conformity… the convenient currency of trust:
With its start in the innocent beginnings of school yards;
The superficial office banter of coffee-breaks,
Or the proclaimed impartiality of laws and their interpretations.

We impose our judgment on mates and playmates:
Our glance, thus more easily placated
by our own features in the bathroom mirror reflection.

Vicious cycle of incestuous thinking:
Where the same begets the same.

And all is well in the filtered cocoon of our private home parties,
Full of repeated rituals…
similar skin tones…
and hair texture.

Similar tastes and social circles,
With the safe ethics from respectable gods.

Society too often comfortable in the toxic fumes of biases,
While floating mines explode,
babies
and toddlers die.

Inconvenient, unsettling facts
and contradictory discoveries
Rendered suspicious…
In the voice and cloth of the Other.

Ignorance and bigotry having too often made impermeable
The veil between such things as…

The freezing death in shipping lanes,
The metallic horror of lung machines,
The inevitability of blue babies…

On one side...
And a happy ending...
on the other.

** Alan Turin, arrested for homosexuality, nevertheless solved the secrets of the World War II German Enigma code; Doctor Salk attacked by anti-Semitism, persevered in his polio research; Vivien Thomas, battled racial prejudice in his work in revolutionary pediatric heart surgery... Examples of persons who bettered the lot of their fellow humans in spite of being considered the Other.

And in fiction (but not less true):

"On making his discovery, the astronomer had presented it to the International Astronomical Congress, in a great demonstration. But he was in Turkish costume, and so nobody would believe what he said.... Grown-ups are like that.... . Fortunately, however, for the reputation of Asteroid B-612, a Turkish dictator made a law that his subjects, under pain of death, should change to European costume. So in 1920 the astronomer gave his demonstration all over again, dressed with impressive style and elegance. And this time everybody accepted his report."
From Le petit prince *by Antoine de Saint Exupéry.*

A City of Two Tales

A night out on the town:
Not much more that a pizza… for an immigrant family.

A young teenager on a mission:
"Be careful crossing!"

A surprisingly warm December:
Some of her friends would be stopping by.

Life and its perils… as it is lived daily,
In this forgettable red-bricked borough.

The tragic… about the tragedies of little people is…
That they are orphaned at their inception:
No one… or nothing, to analyze the intricacies of parenthood.

Not the mother, not the child or the driver
It would not have mattered… It simply had to be so…

Blame a convergence of preordained randomness.

And now… she lies dead in the arms of the one who gave her life:
Had given her twenty dollars… having ordered a proletarian feast,
In this city of excesses.

And so…as it should be, in the universe of jaded streets,
She was killed with her pepperoni treasure.

Her crazed mother too lately cradling her broken body:
Just a police squad car and a sergeant with his own thoughts
about his own children,
Quietly watching the blood hosed into the gutter:
A solitary police car, observing the solitary ritual…

All the dignitaries and media are downtown, preparing for the holidays.

Teenager crosses a dimly lit boulevard of the city, at year-end holiday time.

Winter Sap

Since that darkness that answered his pain
Faint groans of cancerous agony in the next bedroom

Nothing and no-one to help:
Not even the burning distraction of tears on his cheeks

Nothing

The universe was, as Camus had foretold:
Equivalent value between the pathos of a mother's death;
Or the earthy hedonism found on the warmth of Mediterranean rocks.

Nothing would change the blind trajectory of hours.
No reprieve from the intervention of various combinations of stellar dust.

But, waiting in the garden,
Oh! what a glorious… momentary… cottony victory,
Of something over nothing.

A quasi-weeping…
At least in his translation into human emotions,
Of the presence of this winter-sap,
As a memorial to a non-existent tree:

Found in the stubborn Sisyphean defiance of this oozing life,
In the cold wind.

Oozing sap from the stump of pine tree** to the memory of little boy: "If only nature knew how magnificent it can be at times." [unattributed remark]

** Continuation of the poem "The atheist, the tree and nothingness," in Asymptotes at the Limit of Passion, *by Jean-Yves Solinga.*

Musical Score

Homage to Pau Casals' 1936 version of J. S. Bach's Cello Suite 1, 1 Prélude.

Infuriating individuality of notes that will not permit smugness:
Grounded in a philosophical state of assuredness,
Steeped in the blackest of one's life:

A monkish cubicle of a university room,
A father's death… and no other available appellate level:
Finding futility, even in lofty academic constructs.

Leading to the un-impeachable conclusion,
As reliable as any, in the thickest of his calculus texts,
Of the existence of that brick wall at the exit door.

Edifices of his youth built on endless North African dunes
of a grainy black and white Santa Claus:
When parents knew the magic that gave order and unity to the world.

Followed by the eerie silence of crashing illusions:
Part of life's lessons about the flimsiness of things.

Emotional suicide…
Then religious adherence to non-adherence.
Divorce from belief… from non-belief.

Letting oneself go into the vastness of neutrality:
A father's death…
The real… and only giver-of-life… is dead.

A disinterested universe
Is already lapping at the porous foundations
Of the now and ineluctable future blackness.

… And then…
Then… these notes… from the innards of a Volkswagen dashboard.

Not optimism... just solace and solidarity.
Simple and noble… human solidarity.

Reading your own thoughts into the nonverbal, quasi hypnotic sequence of single notes at the introduction of the suite, as a transcription of the inenarrable.

The Spiritual Rhesus Monkey

In homage to Umberto Eco

A spectacular feat of evolution:
The imposition of shame, on a previously simple cycle of life and life-giving.

A label is now ascribed to the natural innocence of a revolving ritual:
That of reproduction… renewal… survival.

Rut… under another name:
Semiotics invading another part of existence.

A place where, an act and its actors, are suddenly struck
—In mid-carnal infraction, and apparently for the first time—
With the spiritual meaning and price of the act in question.

A spiritual overlay imposed on the world of these brighter primates
Amidst the grunting chaos of the jungle and fallen apples.

Henceforth would exist a new value-judgement,
In the pairing between the signifier and signified,
Where none had existed before.

And thus, unlike previous early-Spring-time encounters,
The sight of sanguine flesh, engorged loins,
Submissive arched quarters of his mate
And the mixing of seeds,

The male is now repulsed…
By his gullibility to the female's charms and fertile scent.

Both now… Having taken the measure of their deed:
A cataclysmic fissure, forever opens in time and space.

The world of the temporal having now been introduced
To the eternal price of real happiness.

"Paradise" … this biblical place, filled with metaphors, at the intersection of the duality of mankind where now stand newly constructed living organisms (a man, a woman) that have divinely acquired a consciousness, a spirituality. They [the human couple or Rhesus monkeys] now, "know" that actions have meaning beyond the act itself, under the sign (in this case) of sex.

Letter to Santa Claus

The Atheist's letter to Santa Claus.

Listen, Santa, maybe… you… will understand me better.
I need a favor, but I'm afraid that the Other One won't be as nice to me.

He will judge me. He will scold me.
He will make me feel guilty.

You know: "Don't touch! Don't look at it too closely!"
"Everything that is good… is bad for you."
"Wait… you'll be rewarded latter."
"Sweets, are for latter… you know… we talked about it… Paradise."

———————————————————

But… listen Santa... I want her now in my arms.
I want her one more time, like a gift, against my bare chest.

You know… like in this special place in Paris.
In this threadbare room… and yet so pretty:
Quiet hours under sheets, surrounded by the hustle of the streets.

Happiness for us and misery for others, on the other side of the door:
My very own Flowers of Evil… in short.

But him… the other one… also with a white beard. the Catechism one.
As much immaterial… non-carnal, as you… Santa.

The one… who burdens our conscience with our conscience.
The one… who would like us to be repulsed by the call of flesh.

The one… who tells us to passively look… without envy:
Instead of recognizing true eternity in the lubricity of sight.

The one of… the abstinence of Lent and laws of the Canon.
The one of… denial of simple things that bring happiness.
The one of… the snake whose message was, after all, correct…
because genuinely human.

And of… this woman, with this apple:
Completely naked… her lips engorged with passion.

If I ask the Other One, he will deny me… he will tell me to wait:
Only to learn too late, that nothing was waiting for me there.

Yes! … I know, Santa,
You and God, are no more than human inventions.
But you, at least, offer the keys to the candy shop:
The other has a list of rules that control happiness.

So… Santa, here is the only thing that I would like:
You are more human… less perfect.

You will grant my wish because you already know.
I have no one else.

There is only you… you, or darkness.

Lettre au Père Noël

L'Athée au Père Noël

Dis… Papa Noël, peut être que toi, tu comprendras mieux
Je voudrais quelque chose, mais j'ai bien peur que l'Autre ne sera pas
aussi aimable :

Il me jugera. Il me grondera.
Il me culpabilisera.

Tu sais : « Ne touche pas ! Ne regarde pas trop de près ! »
« Tout ce qui est bon… est mauvais. »
« Attends… tu verras que plus tard, tu seras récompensé. »
« Les sucreries, c'est pour plus tard…tu sais»… on en a parlé… le Paradis. »

———————————————————————

Mais… dis…Papa Noël… je la veux maintenant dans les bras.
Je la veux encore une fois, comme cadeau, contre ma poitrine nue.

Tu connais très bien… cet endroit favori à Paris.
Dans cette pièce vieillotte… et pourtant si jolie :
Des heures tranquilles sous les draps, au milieu du grouillement dans les rues.

Le bonheur pour nous et la misère pour les autres de l'autre côté de la porte :
Mes propres Fleurs du mal… quoi... pour Noel.

Mais lui… l'autre… lui aussi, avec la barbe blanche… celui du Catéchisme,
Tout autant immatériel… non-charnel, comme toi… Père Noël.

Celui… qui alourdit notre conscience avec notre conscience.
Celui… qui voudrait nous rendre froid aux appels de la chair.
Celui… qui nous dit de passivement regarder... sans envies :
Au lieu de reconnaître la vraie éternité dans la lubricité de la vue.

Celui… des abstinences du Carême et des lois du Canon.
Celui… du reniement des choses simples qui rendent heureux.
Celui… du serpent dont le message était pourtant correct… parce
honnêtement humain.

Et de… cette femme, avec cette pomme :
Toute nue et innocente, avec des lèvres engorgées de passion.

Si je demande à l'Autre, il me refusera… il me dira d'attendre :
Pour apprendre trop tard, que finalement rien ne m'y attendait.

Oui… je sais, Père Noël,
Vous et le Bon Dieu, vous n'êtes que des inventions de l'homme.
Mais toi, au moins, tu offres les clefs de la confiserie :
L'autre a la liste des règles qui contrôlent le bonheur.

Alors… voilà, Papa Noël… voilà la seule chose que je voudrais ;
Tu es plus humain… moins parfait… tu exauceras mon vœu.

Car comme tu le sais déjà… je n'ai personne d'autre.
Il n'y a que toi… toi, ou le noir.

Evolved Trickery:**

An alternate Lyrical Reality.

Seeing… deceptive reconstruction:
During… Or after… Long…
Very long after intimate precious moments.

Lasting visions, still now… imprinted on graying lovers.

A conspiracy to appease… to filter… to tease…
With just enough from the original unabridged color palette.

Seemingly based in the very and oh!... so, human necessity,
To stabilize, compose… recreate… To enjoy once more.

Monet having given a painterly permanence,
To unassuming nebulous, water molecules,
Gracefully obeying through their wind-laced tendrils,
The frigidity of gaseous theory.

Evolved trickery… a necessary emotional deceit
Born in the need from the human glance, upon clueless photons:

Themselves, reflections of the un-reality of yesterday and the now.

Thus…
The poet reads passion in the rushing blood,
Under the pinkish elasticity of flesh,
While it hides the vulgar organic reality of corpuscles.

.

** *This poem is a continuation of my "Silky Reality" (in* Asymptotes at the Infinity of Passion, *2015)*

*Continuing discoveries in neuro-sciences, show how humans have evolved into accepting the perceived*** reality of what our eyes capture. And yet, this is the same filtered reality on which artists and writers have based and created their art. Hence this poem, an alternate lyrical reality, inspired by the passage in* Gulliver's Travels, *when the minuscule Gulliver can see all the defects in the nursemaid's huge breasts.*

*** *Human eyes do not see parts of the spectrum and or the image arrives upside down on the retina, etc.…The sight of the woman's breast is repulsive to Gulliver. It is so large in his view that he can see all of its defects.*

The falcon cannot hear the falconer;
Things fall apart; the centre cannot hold;
Mere anarchy is loosed upon the world,
The blood-dimmed tide is loosed, and everywhere
The ceremony of innocence is drowned;
The best lack all conviction, while the worst
Are full of passionate intensity. (W.B. Yeast)

Emergency Room Nurse

Inconsolable women,
Violated once in a side street
And now,
With a rape kit and prodding questions.

Mute children… too young and innocent
To know the vocabulary that would describe their despair.

Mutilated bodies of gang wars and flying metal.

Late night surrealistic show, on a stage of blood soaked sheets:
Endless non-scripted plots of entrances, stage left.

Arbitrary endings of evenhanded misery and cruelty
Worthy of the Caligula of Camus.

Unfolding last act,
In vapors of calming opiates.

———————————————

Yet… at times… somehow…
The mind knows how to protect the soul for its future.

Thus, protecting the center of things
From the gravitational attraction of surrounding evil.

Steamy thoughts,
While applying a plaster cast under harsh medical lights,
About steamy moments…
Under steamy sheets, full of acrid scents of hedonism.

Escapist mental reconstructions
Of the original beauty of a disfigured face,
Or the puppy glance of a hand-cuffed teenager.

And then… and then…
This poetic paradisiacal plunge into a sensual refuge,
A world that counteracts immediate horrors:
Anchoring the soul into a livable past and hopeful future.

White hot verbalization,
Emanating from this apparently stern professional,
Having managed to keep alive the fire that drives human passions.

Urban hospital emergency-room nurse who, despite the nightly horrors of her job, managed, in her down time, to write lines of elegantly steamy, personal lyricism in her poetry.

The Simplicity of Kindness

Nineteenth century romantic literature invades the present.

Her tainted reputation had reached him,
Along with relevant identifying skills and habits:
Like entries on some police post-mortem log.

All he ever saw was her distance... her nobility:
The unquestioned beauty of her persona
And the repulsive treatment associated with her flesh.

Boozy university bullshit sessions on the fourth floor.
Neanderthal ambiance of rumors.
Glorification of the chase and capture,
In an academic Savannah of hapless preys.

She had always been, in his mind, a high priestess:
Protected by the invisible thorns of protocols,
As she sat with hints of haughty inner-sadness.

And now... this awkward silence and their respective faraway glances.
Chance meeting in downstairs waiting space...
And the obligation of obligatory banter.

Like for some delusional teenager, his reading world of Freshman literature,
Had predicted the presence of such explosive shortcuts
Straight into the purified spaces that inhabit pure human emotions.

And thus...
Unknown and unknowable things were said and hinted,
In the simplicity of natural unrehearsed moments,

Encapsulated, upon her leaving and whispering over her shoulder,
In a gentle grateful smile.

"Thank you... for having been so kind to me."

An apparently unapproachable university sorority queen 'with a scandalous reputation,' after an unlikely conversation with a 'lowly general-population' student during a tête-à-tête in the waiting room of a dormitory.

Sacred Fire

Rosebud: *Voice-over from Citizen Kane.*

Hellish breath of street machinery,
Hammering noise from blackish oiled steel-entrails of compressors.

Ambient anti-human… non-human scenery
Of urban inorganic desert:

His…
dying-place.

———————————————————

Distantly cold professionalism of emergency attendant,
Cooling flesh on porous cement sidewalk…

And that imperceptible movement of the lips,
Accompanied by otherworldly exhaled syllables:

The same spoken in the illuminated moments
of mankind's illuminated women and men of history
from their last breath in this universe.

A magic silence fell all around,
When the paramedic heard
"Flower of Paradise."

Like embers of the sacred fire of prehistoric tribes:
Iconic words that she would knowingly carry henceforth
In the protective gentleness in her soul.

A medic had told her that one of the E.M.T.'s had distinctly heard enigmatic words from the lips of her companion, as he lay dying among the urban chaos. It was: "Flower of Paradise."

Reconstructing Mirages

Inspired by The Kiss, *by Auguste Rodin.*

Their first kiss:
The foundation of their private world.

There… at the beginning…
The quasi-religious icon of their genesis,
In an otherwise secular, hedonistic moment.

The supremely human act of trembling flesh
Captured by artists in the solidity of museum white marble.

It will become their polar night-star
In the otherwise meanders of daily living:

Bringing him…
Bringing her…
Bringing them…
Back to the micro-second before closing their eyes:
Keeping instinctively the same heading toward the other's lips.

Towards a galactic explosion
Made of preceding eons of intimacies found in vaporous stellar clouds.

Leaving the poet, feverishly attempting to reconstruct
The already scattering molecules of happiness.

Trepidation by poets, upon reading the scientific recurring evidence that our human memories are no more that chemical changes to our brain. Thus, souvenirs of our most precious moments being no more than organic chemical chains of processes in one of our organs.
What are, the poetic implications concerning this, the most iconic subject of lyricism [the first kiss between future lovers] since it seems that the very act of trying to remember details of past events, modifies them?

Night-Flight

To die with recalcitrance.
But die nevertheless.

To die with every living fibers on life's side.
But die nevertheless.

To die with images of hidden contortions of swaying hips
Under the luscious quasi transparent black silk
Of a minimal dress.

But die nevertheless…
With illusions of unending continuity:
Such as the tactile presence of the index on the cosmic replay button.

Listening to Pascal Dubois- Nula (Night-flight Mix).

Odd Couple

Homage to The Plague, *by Albert Camus.*

Academic office:
Akin to the iconic fields of battle among the pages
Of their personally penned textbooks.

These man-made concepts of aggressions:
With their forgotten genesis
And embittered endings.

Never a lack of source…:
Philosophical bifurcations of needs and whims.
Obsessions and drives.
Weaknesses and aspirations.

Mindless disagreements, repeated and repeatable mass killing.

And throughout our learned men
Retaining their very own thin-skinned sentiments.

Like two school-yard boys:
Wincing while shaking hands.

And then… somehow…
Gentle and unseen fertile seeds settled into the interspaces of their words

Followed by
Genuine laughter and good-natured derision:
Un-academic back-slapping humor.

Even some hints of a squint of approval,
Generously sprinkled with cultural repartees.

When this oblique reference… the imminent death of one…
Transformed the controlled wetness in their eyes
Into the noblest gesture in front of a common enemy:

Unspoken basic human solidarity.

Circumstances put reciprocally disdainful former university colleagues back into necessary close proximity. The medical prognostic of one modifies their deep seated and divergent learned views of each other's life style and politics.

Musical Addiction

To Mick Jagger: Finding once more the exhilaration of youth through a musical beat.

Ah! To forever feel the teasing, lush hesitation
Of the double... triple syncopated cascades...

From the snare drum and its obedient synthetic skin,
Then unto its viscerally answered echoes... on hers.

From the halting bass drum.
Left/right oscillation of rejuvenated curvature of the hips,
To the musical palpitations of a new found younger heart.

Alchemic irrationality of the heat and beat of the music.
Hammering notes peeling the insulating dusty layers off of the soul:

Revealing the raw sanguine bare flesh of virility
Still remaining underneath.

Rediscovery of that hypersensitivity,
To life and its moments.

Natural ease of unrestrained,
Unforced sensuality:

Sexuality found in the morsels of life... simply by living it once more.

Like a modern day Titan:
Extracting sweet sugary pleasures
From the depth of earthy nourishments,

Rediscovered in the crimson folds of pliable flesh.

Seventeen minutes into "Lounge Café: TAO Lounge Music Beats."

Laughter and Tears

A clown among us,
This disarticulated Other… a chameleon of emotions.

Aristocratic sadness behind the face.
An image of humanity's tender side… in front of history's ugliest.

Apparently fearless
In mocking mortal demons of prejudices.*

Becoming a face for those
Oppressed and dispossessed.

Magically making the inorganic flatness on the screen
Invade our vision in the visceral… fourth dimension.

Thus making once again…
Language … laughter and tears
The classical tongue of the universal condition.

With pieces of ourselves on display
As predicated since the sun-bleached scenes
Of Grecian theaters.

Tears among the raucous laughter,
In the dead-star effect of his charcoal glance,

Pulling the viewer deep into an incestuous marriage
Of the tragic and ridiculous:

Giving the pathetic the incongruous elegance
Of an ill-fitted jacket in a top-hat,

Somehow able to redeem…
The Tramp… Poverty and… the Outsider.

Inspired by the scene, in Au revoir les enfants *by Louis Malle, when the camera pans over the precious moments of laughter caused by the antics of Charlie Chaplin in the shadows of impending doom of occupied France during World War II.*

* *With the* Immigrant *(among other movies and other personal characteristics) Charlie Chaplin could not come back to the United States for years.*

Just a Measuring Stick on the Wall

Was it the very insignificance of the door jamb?

These markings hiding in plain sight,
Between the kitchen smells and the back yard entry?

Between mom's moist cinnamon buns?
And the dog's sleeping blanket?

The everyday of things:
Their unassuming value and easy accessibility?

To touch?
Sight?
And smells?

The repeated repetition of routine?
The muddy paw prints? Motherly scolding for disappearing sweets?

The softness of the process of life and growing up,
Indexed into the pliable wood of time.

Parents having solemnly taken out the family carving knife:
The one for iconic turkeys and crown roasts…

… Used now for this special ceremony full of the ritual of exclamations
At the concrete evidence of growth toward manhood,

Having somehow taken place
Within the clutter of after school activities and school dances;
Heartbreaks and emergency rooms visits;
Diplomas and careers to fulfill.

This house… now having emptied itself of its best
For the benefit of life outside:

Leaving behind traces of a past
Imprinted into horizontal timelines memories.

Retiring couple moving out of their house, looking at the kitchen door jamb with the scratches showing their now adult son's growth from boyhood.

"I Have Lost the Courage…"

"I have lost the courage
To see you again:
That is my best proof of my love for you…"

The jagged-edge elements of daily life and living.
Crazed hours of crammed entries in calendars.
Erasures and reschedules on wrinkled agenda
Multiplicity of antiseptic glass and stainless steel airports
Followed by night-concierge desks.

Vaulted medieval lecture halls and now lonely hotel views of Paris rooftops.
Accompanying transparent memories of her form
Under black cocktail dresses.

Increasing distance and time
Between the grounding earthy presence of her flesh
And fewer interventions from these gods
Found in their own research-writings for mythology textbooks.

Searching for an intersection in space and time
For these two wandering souls
To collide in the accelerator of granted wishes

In this corner of the universe and same hotel room
Protected from prying eyes and prying mates

"I have lost the courage to see you again:
That is my best proof of my love for you"

_____

Successful, traveling academics having to end their relationship

… "What makes me worthy of you…
…IS… what makes me turn away from your love."
The world of literature had once more invaded his reality.
"I want to kiss you all over… and over again…"
…which now disappears in the ambient noise of his conscience."

Inspired by Le Cid *by Pierre Corneille [from* Clair-Obscur of the Soul *2008, by Jean-Yves Vincent Solinga]*

Heavenly Highway

The winds had changed: the calendar speeds up in these hills
Last night's warmth was a last gasp.

The drying leaves mimicked shivering.
The blanching blades of grass made for a hushed chorus:
Whispering tales of killing cold and pellets of snow.

Inviting this hardened man's heart to enter the gigantic equation
Of the submission of things to nature's unrelenting and unstoppable cycles:
Those of life and the cruelty of leaving it all behind…

…. So it seemed in his mind,
Juxtaposed like a double exposure of very different films:
Becoming just an extension of the urban canvas of his routine.

Self-anointed immortal teenagers, separated from their heads
In the mangle of metal.
Twelve-year-old children exploded into pieces in crosswalks.

The steady hand of the universe handing out its sentences
With equally cool disdain:

Pregnant women or drug pushers
All making their appearance in his reports.

Was it the totality of these recurring visions
Dancing on the polished rifle telescope that made him lower the crosshairs?

Thus, for once, "Damn it" … playing God,
By letting an arrogantly beautiful adult deer
Impregnate his part of eternity into a nearby willing mate.

Seasoned N.Y.P.D. highway cop, in upstate New York woods in the early fall.

Guilt's Antechamber

One can only wonder,
if
In the totality of the misery that had spun
Around the blackness of the black star that he had been,

One can only wonder
if
For an infinitesimal flash of human conscience,
Interspaced in the surviving morsels of human flesh that bore him,

One can only wonder,
if
The dying glance of unconditional love from this beast
Chased the monstrous double ganger from his dead heart:

Allowing a troubled little boy, he once was
To feel guilt once more.

It was reported that Hitler made sure that the cyanide used by his mistress was still effective by giving it first to his dog.

Guilt and Possibilities

Reflections and flashbacks of a post-World War II survivor upon reaching New York City harbor.

Colliding currents in the swirls of existence:
Treating life, death and survival
Like so much ink scratches on balance sheets.

This instant... or the next one
This man or another

Such a seemingly miniscule reserve of good,
Among the malignancy of evil.

The anonymity of acts
And their apparently worthless importance.

And so... it is done
He will die... I will live
For another day... or a life

The Injustice... the damnable unjustified equivalency of outcomes:
His for mine
My survival... for his demise.

And no one the wiser in the putrid smells of dying flesh.
Insane guard dogs and crazier handlers.
Acrid clouds of carbonized humans
And apocalyptic and phantasmagoric figures.

The Darwinism of survival of the camps
And above it all... the silence of divine indifference.

And all that is left for the ultimate survivors
Is the everlasting weight of the universe on their shoulders.

———————————————————

On the steps of a New York dock:
With the kitchen smells of transplanted cultures;
One week's worth of money in his pocket

And both tears and stars in his eyes.

A misspelled stamped official identification
And the early-dew of the Hudson.

A shy foggy-gray Statue of Liberty.
A visceral need to do good things with his life.

All of these things... All these emotions...
Strangely centered in his rushing heart:
Joyfully sending the sap of energy into his being.

Not unlike the transplant recipient,
With someone else's organ:

He takes his first deep new breath
Upon reaching the door of his destiny,

Acknowledging next to his heart the fertile noises of the living,
With a wise gulp of sadness.

Inspired by the scene of the Dutch movie Winter in Wartime, *where Micheil's father refuses the offer to be replaced by another villager; thus leading to his being shot by the Nazis.*

And on a very personal note, by my mother's refusal, after the fighting, to sign the arrest papers and inevitable firing squad death of a Vichy French officer who had turned my father's name to the Gestapo. "I don't want your husband on my conscience," she said to his sobbing wife.

This thought-poem-experiment reflects upon these existentialist moments imposed by horrifying wartime circumstances.

Great Evils and Greater Salvation

Post World War One : Quai de Rive Neuve, Marseille, France.

Welcoming warmth of cellulose.
The intoxicating acrid earthy scent of leather spines.
Multicolored world of alignment of names.

Names!
Disciplined height of folios
Forming a tabernacle with side chapels of reading nooks:
Always entered with quasi-religious reverence.

Imprisoned between the docks and poverty.
Loneliness and abandonment.
Coldness and survival.

Returning ghosts of returning neighbors:
Survivors of hellish cruelty,
Of a mindless apocalypse.

Interspaced by glimpses of provençal sun:
Caught in an existence of beauty
And the cruelty of existence.

We are correct to wonder…
If the universe does indeed acknowledge such pivotal moments
With welcomed shivers of apprehension:

That moment… that noble moment…

When good is happening
Amidst all that denies it.

When basic human happiness
Squeezes into the interspaces of misery.

That moment… of dampness on the bedroom walls,
Decrepit hall, nauseating smells of decaying fish,
Abused wives, cheap red wine and white nights,

Blank stares at blank futures from disembarking Neapolitans,
In a present barely past the destruction of worlds:
And its chlorine gas consequences.

Then…What a light!…
Piercing and benign,

Fertile light… upon unblinking eyes:
Opening the deep-grained chestnut-wood door!

A sanctuary for new things and people.
Places and feelings.

For kingly decisions. Heroic deeds.
And heartbreaking treasons.

Descriptions of solidarity and emotions.
Comrades and mortal enemies.

Great evils and greater salvation.
Paradisiacal and hellish state of mind
Over turquoise waves.

The smell of spices.
And intriguing strangeness of the Other.

The smell of spices.
And intriguing strangeness of the Other.

Inspired by my father, Marcel Laurent Solinga and his years as a foster child in the early part of the twentieth century. A local saintly parish priest took him in, at which time my father was introduced to the escapist world of books in the priest's private library.*

Among others, he had read practically all of Honoré de Balzac. Victor Hugo and Alexandre Dumas by his early teen age years.

* With some poetic license.

Paris : Demi-sommeil *

La bohème

…Souvent il m'arrivait
Devant mon chevalet
De passer des nuits blanches
Retouchant le dessin
De la ligne d'un sein
Du galbe d'une hanche
Et ce n'est qu'au matin
Qu'on s'asseyait enfin
Devant un café crème
Épuisés mais ravis
Fallait-il que l'on s'aime…
Et qu'on aime la vie ("La bohème" by Charles Aznavour)

The invisible alien army
　　　　of street cleaners already at work

The hesitant rebirth
　　　　of crazed buzzing of vélomoteurs

Crystalline clinking sound
　　　　of espresso porcelain cups being lined up on
　　　　　　the zinc bar

Habitués
　　　　still arguing last night's off-side

The minutia of life
　　　　starting to invade the routine of living

————————————————

When his left arm
　　　　reconfirmed her absence in his bed

Torture
　　　　of organic and floral hints of her on
　　　　　　wrinkled sheets

Fleeting thoughts
　　　　about Adam tearfully looking back
　　　　　　at gates of Paradise

"Waking up in Saint Germain des prés"
First published in the Peacock Journal *

Jellified Souvenirs

At the beginning there was…
God's index transferring life.
And with it, consciousness.

Michelangelo's attempt to codify how we know… that we know,
Using the warm colors of humanism.

And now, the harsh brightness, under hospital lights,
Where the tip of the surgeon's scalpel is entering the molecular brain matter.

In between exists mankind's dashed hope
Of lyrically stopping time in time:

That would try to encapsulate our first kiss
With the talented alchemy of the arts:

Perpetuating its presence.
Extending that moment of embrace
Into echoes of remembrance.

All this romanticized universe dashed,
In the realization that memories of warm summer afternoons,
Swoons of ecstasy, a mother's calming hug,
A smiling kindergarten class,
Are just imprints on jellified molecules,

Oozing out on the doctor's steady hands,
In a chorus of indifferent heart monitors.

Mounting evidence that what we conceive as our reality of memories is no more than cerebral molecules.

Rosebud

No one could fathom the reason for his presence there:
A deadly cold New England morning,
The ones so symbolically negative when compared to the warmth of his
Maghreban youth.

Why this miniscule pond: next this miniscule mill?
Why not his preferred lyrical demise in a Parisian seventh floor?

What of this death in the anti-thesis of what he craved?
Even foregoing the artificial warmth of a chimney fire?

Why this alignment of his body, perpendicular to the frozen shore:
Seemingly overseeing a microcosm of the frigid flatness of eternity.

Upon the ambulance arrival,
Hands neatly crossed over his chest in mummified acceptance,
What of this cryptic last whisper in the E.M.T.'s ear…
"Flower of Paradise?"

Reflections on the iconic last word of the protagonist in Citizen Kane: Rosebud.
Nota bene: this poem has the same inspiration as "Sacred Fire."

African Diamonds

Harden to stone-hard clarity:
Survivors of survivors.

Black songbirds of color blind human passions

Human emotions
Having traveled well in the bowels of inhuman ships,
To flower in our midst:
Reminding all of us of a communality
Under our quivering skin cells.

Homage to William de Vaughn, Curtis Mayfield and so many other Afro-American artists and their gift of musical smoothness to the American culture.

Title is also inspired by the lethal African-diamond trade.

Aging Man-of-the-World

It had always seemed so easy... too easy in retrospective.
Boulevardier… it was said of his past conquests.

There was an instinctive ease.
The one associated with natural talents in sports:
Evolution giving free reins to winning instincts.

It was there from the start. Raw… but all in place.
A little awkward at first, but good student of his simmering talents.

Flexible with difficult relationships: Never imposing himself.
Exhibiting the disarming submissive hesitation of a little boy well into
adulthood.

Never having a particular goal for the evening:
Thus, often pleasantly surprised at its end.

Like the parlors game of past societies,
Self-assured while knowing being watched.
Tested and retested for decorum and respect.
People just liked being with him.

And then… unusual apparitions of voids in otherwise pleasant soirées.
Inattention to too many of his witticisms.
Repeated corrections… now… of past ignored infractions.

A lateness in the reaction to his touch.
A distraction in her glance from around the room:
He felt off-stage: his spotlight dimming.

They had walked in their favorite restaurant…
… She was two steps in front.

*He felt like an old brave soldier: worthy of patronizing respect; but no longer the subtle
signs of acknowledgment of his presence in the sensuality of interpersonal rituals.*

Between Le Sacré Cœur and La Place Blanche

Hommage à Charles Baudelaire

Duality of this woman and this city:
Up high on the soil of martyrs,
Urban Virgin... Protected in Byzantine whiteness.

Modern-day sufferers of all sorts of afflictions still crawling at your feet,
Trembling in the trove of feverish passions of the flesh and soul:
Sanguine stigmata hidden and exposed.

Duality of this woman:
Urbanized Holy Virgin. Lady of stylish office suits,
Creased white blouses with hints of black lace support.
Un-approachable creature of city life,
In her habitat and predatory glance.

Duality in this woman:
An urban contemporary holy virgin
With the idealized attributes:
Lady of the untouchable and non-approachable qualities.

All the iridescence of Temple Vestals.
Draped incarnation of thoughts and desires,
In this majestic reclining presence in a miniscule bed
Whose ethereal nudity
Would have tested the choices of paint mounds on the palette.

Leaving the artist paralyzed, in his ambivalence,
Between his allegiance to the wealth of the double nature of the subject
And the idealization of her flesh:
Still sparkling in fresh images of hedonism
And earthy essences from the heights of ecstasy.

Overlapping images of Paris incarnated in the same woman.

Duality

The definition of the untouchable ideal:
From the inception of their relationship.

An appearance... an organic comportment
Of the nobility of ease:
Akin to the textbook royalties of his lectures.

A polished marbly, impervious exterior,
Protecting a cocooned emotional interior.

He had sensed that her stony façade,
Was an instinctive protection against the subtle cruelties
Of gritty cocktail reception mannerisms.

Resulting in thick scars of survival
In the sanguine warfare of the heart.

Grande dame of societies
Of acceptable and despicable behaviors,

Of the intricacies
And dead-ends of dangerous liaisons,

She wore a suit of armor
Through her travels on several continents.

It was upon her coming back to his minuscule Parisian room
Honored... now... by her strewn Dior silk undergarments

That she knowingly... languishingly...
Let him gaze at her alleged imperfection...

[Otherwise easily concealable with a simple wrinkling of the bed sheets]

… Superbly… silently…
Entrusting him with ownership of the surprising fragile lacy quality
And persistent virginal lyricism
Of her soul.

Precious moment of a 'Sentimental Education' when the protagonist is finally allowed entry into the very susceptibly of another.

Inspired, in particular, by passages of La nouvelle Héloïse *of Jean-Jacques Rousseau and* La chartreuse de Parme *by Stendhal.*

Grains of Sand

Homage to Jacques Prévert, "les feuilles mortes" [by Yves Montand] and Hall & Oats, "One on one."

They were all there... each in their respective place and role:
Youth, passion, unregulated minutes and pliable future.

Slow-burn of inception in an intimate stellar birthing.
Gentle falsetto of musical pearls,
Rhythmically wrapped by knowing fingers on bass strings:
Echoing magic of unfathomable depth,
Born from undefined but very real yearnings.

Seemingly limitless expansion
Of how art and artists can challenge
The selfish Hellenistic gods at their game...

...By humanly exuding sparkles of divine emanation of lubricity.
Thus...forever sprinkling the firmament
With the grainy memory of their steps,
left by ex-lovers, on sands of time past.

Unattributed comment about the instantaneous recollection of memories associated with music: "... the synesthesia induced by accidentally and painfully listening to a song that seemingly makes every synopsis of one's brain uncontrollably recreate the couch, the embrace, the snapping of the static sparks on the vinyl .... And... her invading glance."

Summer Peaches

Did the optics irritate built-in sensitivities?
Did universal standards of decency... trigger some uneasiness?

Was it the grand fatherly stoop... of the back of the servant... when serving?
Was it the incongruity of the ebony deep of the wrist... showing through
the slit in the virginal white of the cotton glove?

Was it because the General
had just been correcting grandiose statements...
of revolutionary claims... of statehood and American emancipation...
producing sour echoes of hypocrisy against the fancy wallpaper?

Did images of horrible generational injustices flash,
Along with a knot of sadness, as he whispered:
"Thank you" for his serving of sweet summer peaches?

The elasticity and evolution of ethics: Picturing a General Washington being served by one his slaves.

Folds in the Cloth of Time

Professors respectively teaching mythology... and then... living it.

Pain... akin to a celestial punishment,
Found in their academic lectures.

A knowing last glimpse upon each other,
As though, they had expected the inevitability of this moment.

As though, the perfect alignment of lyrical forces,
Had provoked the envy from those jaded, sleepy, mythological gods of
their textbooks.

The selfish hold on happiness, from some of the divinities,
Somehow threatened by these mere mortals,
seated at a café, place Clichy.

The reciprocal glance of this couple
Creating a crease, a fold... in the cloth of time and space.

The very fragility of their embrace,
Their very awareness of being loved,

Now enviously recognized as such
By the nihilistic universe.

It is thus, at the instant of separation,
That we find the origins of the tears cried by universal lovers:

The consequence of glorified human happiness,
Found In the eternal glance of Renoir,
The play of light on nubile flesh,
The pliability of white marble of Rodin,
The sinful joy of a remorseful Baudelaire...

Observed by…
Multi-colored nebulae,
The creamy Milky Way cloud,
And the darkness of black holes:

All part of a cosmological Elysium that does not long condone
This privileged space formed around earthly lovers.

University academics saying their farewells in the face of end of life diagnosis of one of them.

Great Blue Heron in Paris

Between Monet's Nymphéas and revolutionary passions
Floating placid leafiness and sanguine virility

Pastel secrets of the palette
And codified political freedoms:
Visions and thoughts now solidified in neoclassical granite.

While on its fragility,
This bird unknowingly honors this setting
With nervous glances full of life and living.

Full of the now and the next meal:
A continuation of things within things
That strangely coexist in fruitful harmony
In an absurd concert of
Mopeds, horns and history.

Strange presence of this strange beast:
Iconic visitor looking up momentarily from the surface,
Towards its ancestors immortalized
In the golden colors of the stone
Of the Luxor obelisk.

Great blue heron at the pond of the Tuileries gardens: Incongruous presence of this animal among the splendors of the past; L'Orangerie, on the left, where Monet's "Nymphéas" are found and, on the right, le Jeu de paume, site of the "Serment du jeu de paume," immortalized by Jacques-Louis David, when French revolutionary fervor gave birth to republican rights.

Solar Memories

The Statue of Liberty, in her green patina and a cold fog at her feet,
Had given him shivering premonitions of changes:

The banality of warmth,
Replaced by freezing toes in paper thin New England tenement
And the envy of a classmate's central heating.

It seemed to explain the hint of sadness in his heart,
Years later, in his spacious warm home office,

When viscerally reminded
Of the value paid by his parents… for his entrance on the Hudson.

Remembering path from passing by Ellis Island to comfortable life in New World.

Ad Vitam Aeternam or Maybe Sooner

Hommage to François Villon's: "La ballade des pendus."
And Alfred de Musset: "Rolla."

The irritating smugness, of those among us,
Who have declared themselves or been anointed at ease with the universe.

The gray uniformity of knowing, whence they came
And to where they are going.

Like rich little boys and girls:
Born so… with no knowledge of the value of the gold in their pockets.

Knowing that nothing or no one can take it:
Being alive… knowing it… and expecting it so:
Ad vitam aeternam.

But, what of those
Who in the middle of divine earthy happiness;
Those who do fight for the moment;
Those who know of the precious ephemeral struggle… of the struggle;

Those who, in the depth of debauchery, can't keep themselves from
looking up:

Having kept pure ingots of righteousness in their soul;
and thus,
Understanding the value of the bipolar duality of our humanity.

So… sleep well François
In your cell, as you await the hangman's noose.

Sleep well Alfred
As your alter ego, Rolla, cries for pieces of his primordial decency
In the youthful warmth of a prostitute.

The bad little good boys in each, is the universal in all:
Giving solidarity to tragedy.

That nagging feeling, that it could be one of us on the stage,
In a continuing presence of ourselves,
Propelled by art… the artist and human passions.

Nocturnal

She had awakened him from deep sleep;
A state, akin to the unquestioning peace of death.

The mindless happiness of nothingness.
No reaching for the frustration of the vaporous.
Today's yearning the same as yesterday.

It was at first, a gentle stroke of her cool fingers on his forehead.
A circular rubbing of his temples:

The same soothing maternal touch, as during the surrealist visions
of the tropical fevers of his youth

Barely audible whispers of his name… his nickname:
A motherly habit for such times.

And then…
like an electric charge… eyes wide opened…
Searching the darkness of the bedroom,
She was gone…

Having left behind the first precious verse,
Capturing, like glassy-ambers -from the depth of the earth-
Her pink sinuous presence,
Under the scented maritime pines of l'Estaque
In the solar hedonism of a lazy afternoon.

Nighttime visit by 'Beauty'.

Einstein... and Beyond

Tell us... what did you see beyond the space and time barrier?
Why did you chose, such a benevolent, sly glance,
Upon your return to us... mere mortals?

Shouldn't it have been, instead, the severe look of the Christ
Having come back from death?*

Should we... rather... chose your fatherly appeasement?
A cosmic way of showing the resignation of not knowing...
Of not ever daring to know?

Like the ephemeral warmth
Of a father's coarse overcoat, around his son's shoulders,
Can either action improve our destiny?

Is the message... in the final analysis... from the ones who know,
That we would be better off by demanding from each other?

By simply holding on to what Camus had learned
On the football fields of his youth:

That camaraderie in the collective effort,
May be... all there is... or ever will be.

Overlapping, of Henryk Ross's photographs of the Lodz ghetto and the deportation of Jewish families in the process of being sent to the extermination camps, with children being held protectively close to their parents; and reflecting upon a photograph of Einstein with those iconic, washed-out, dreamy eyes.

* Reference to "Nuptials," in the passage "Desert," by Albert Camus: ... upon coming out of his tomb, the rising Christ by Piero della Francesca does not have the look of a man. No happiness is seen in his glance—but rather a wild and soulless greatness on his face, that I cannot stop from taking as a resolution to live. For the wise like the idiot expresses little. (Translation by Jean-Yves Solinga)

GLOSSARY

Absurdism: The general philosophical position that there is a disharmony between life [the awareness of life] and death [or its awareness]. Also, the general belief that therefore there is no divine direction to our existence, [See Albert Camus, Jean-Paul Sartre among others]

Baudelaire, Charles: poet ["the flowers of evil"] combining explosive sensibility of self-analysis and attraction to self-destruction. [see François Villon and Alfred de Musset] [see la Place Blanche]. Known in French literature texts as one of the "damned" writers for his troubles life style and personality, but like his fellow authors, with a consciousness of his weaknesses. He is the writer of the urban setting: Paris. His only ventures to the Caribbean world through "reveries" and finds inspiration in the arms of a prostitute of this faraway exotic world.

Booz endormi [the sleep of Boas] In which Victor Hugo, beautifully describes divine machination in making the night sky… "nuptial."

Bled: Moroccan term for the country side.

Caesar [of Camus]: Reference in this text to the play "Caligula" by Albert Camus, where the playwright uses the capricious and sadistic Roman emperor as an example of we could call destiny or fate. Also, from his earliest "notebooks" writings, Camus, who had been an avid football player, liked the concrete example of solidarity that this team sport offered [even or especially in a losing result. i.e. the Myth of Sisyphus].

Cartesian skepticism: [see René Descartes] French philosopher [of Cogito ergo sum, fame] and mathematician [Cartesian coordinates] believer in human rational thinking.

Chartreuse de .Parme [la]: Nineteenth century novel by Stendhal with subtle analysis of what is known as sentimental education.

Confit: Duck or goose part that have macerated in their own fat. In the context of the poem, this culinary ingredient [rare and expensive, before modern storage] is used in the poem as the ultimate sign of faith in this housewife's mind of the resilience of her family and the village with German soldiers in the village.

Courbet: French painter whose "La naissance du monde" says everything about what passion for life can look like. His realistic style and some of his themes are still breathtakingly important.

Dali, Salvador: My dedication to Dali in "Blue Metallic Swan" is the obvious delirium that affected me in that tropical fever. However, here again, I overlap the after effects of chloroform, in another event, after a broken arm operation in my youth.

"Death of the author" [see Nouvelle critique and Roland Barthes]:
The Nouvelle critique movement [and the section that I use in this text] is difficult to explain; but here is an excellent start from Wikipedia: "The essay "The Death of the Author" can have several implications, both literal and metaphoric. In literary criticism, the death of the Author is the "death" of the physical real-life author of the work: For example, Baudelaire's "The Flowers of Evil" should not be analyzed in the context of Baudelaire's life. In literary writing, the death of the Author is the "death" of the omniscient narrator and the author who calls attention to his presence in the text. For example, the author should not address the readers with phrases such as "dear reader"; the author should not give information about the characters that cannot be known in a "real-life" situation—such as characters' thoughts and feelings. Another example is the use of "I" from the point of view of the author. The death of the Author is the inability to create, produce, or discover any text or idea. The author is a "scriptor" who simply collects preexisting quotations. He is not able to create or decide the meaning of his work. The task of meaning falls "in the destination"—the reader."

Fèz: A religious city in Morocco, restricted to non-Muslims. These 'religious cities' have remained mysterious for outsiders thus surrounded by an aura of mysticism: Late nineteenth century account of Europeans who had visited under these sites in disguise came back with descriptions of a culture and times that fed literature and Hollywood for decades.

Hawking, Steven: His attempts to make his audience understand our place in the universe from a scientific view point. ["Microbial Thoughts"] [see Blaise Pascal].

Habitué(s): "Regular" clients of a café establishment.

Hugo Victor: In *Notre Dame de Paris* he managed to turn the cathedral into a living thing: Defining the city forever. It is Hugo that I have in mind to describe the richness of shadows in "Flâner dans Paris."

Madame Bovary: In this text, a "woman" emotionally and miserably unsuited for her times and society. [see Marie Antoinette]

Maghreb: Arabic for the "setting sun." The land farthest West in North Africa (Morocco).

Marquis de Sade: His reputation as a pornographer unfortunately overwhelms his contribution in freeing modern thought, pushing back cultural and religious restrictions, and themes.

Marie Antoinette: In this text, a different perspective on this "child/woman" pigeon-holed by history into almost a caricature of film directors' fantasies. My poem sees her, instead, constrained by circumstances and rebelling in her personal behavior, as her womanhood refuses to be extinguished. [see Madame Bovary]

Meknès: Holy city in Morocco: Usually restricted to non-Muslims. [see Fèz]

Montmartre: The Mount of Martyrs. A hill overlooking Paris, whose beginnings are soaked in the blood of early Christians slaughtered for their steadfast beliefs: Ironically becoming the iconic center of Can-Can dancers. Toulouse Lautrec. Ever the city of contrasts: le Sacré Coeur basilica has now replaced the martyrs' crucifixion crosses. [see la Place Blanche]

Nouvelle critique [la]: A radical literary school of the latter part of the 20th century and its view of the author, the reader and the text [see Roland Barthes]. For the purpose and space of the introduction of this book I have broached how I have weaved some of the views of this literary movement into my views of the writer as the physical presence, in time and space, and the author [the name on the front cover], and the space or lack of space in between the two. This is the subject I approach in dealing with "the Muse" in the preface. After years of studying literature and these topics I find myself a complete non-believer with a clean conscience: I don't care. I just want to use everything and anything, real or imaginary to inspire. But the poems have to be written by someone: So here they are.

Nouvelle Héloïse[la]: A subtle analysis of human emotions and sentimentality—in particular femininity—by Jean-Jacques Rousseau. [Part of a late eighteenth century, early nineteenth century movement in Europe known as the Roman personnel, whose influence I still use in poems such as "Canaries in the Coal Mines."

Pascal, Blaise: French philosopher, who asked wide ranging questions about mankind's status in a huge universe [the "Thinking Reed"] from a religious angle. [see "Microbial Thoughts"] see Steven Hawking.

Place Blanche [la]: Is known for its hedonistic night life. [le Moulin Rouge] [see Montmartre] contrasted in this text with the religious symbol at the top of the hill, represented by the gloriously, white-stone Sacré Coeur basilica.

Plan de Cuque: A little town north east of Marseille where my parents, sister and brother, experienced the dangerous last days of the liberation of Southern France when the line of demarcation changed daily and the French population was susceptible to reprisals from both sides. In this text I overlapped some of the war scenes from earlier ones in the war, in Corsica.

Rolla: A very powerful mixture of hedonism, fatalism and surprising self-searching morality in this long poem by Alfred de Musset: Portraying a débauché who will eventually commit suicide at the end of the night, in the arms of a young prostitute.

Sacré Coeur [le]: Basilica at the top of the "mount of martyrs" [Montmartre] [Place Blanche] overlooking Paris. At its feet, is located the historic night life of the city. [see Baudelaire]

Sahel: A large swath of landmass bordering the Sahara.

Sidi Moussa: Lord Moses in Arabic. The author refers to the name as well as the beach, by the same name, near Salé, in Morocco. It is a place of lyrical return in his poetry.

Stendhal: Nineteenth century novelist with an uncanny and subtle description of human and in particular feminine emotions. [see la Chartreuse de Parme]

Vercors ["Morsels of Hope"]: Pseudonym for the author [Jean Bruller] of *Le silence de la mer*: Powerful statement of unbending pride by a defeated French family during German occupation. The "let's eat" remark, is an echo, in a previous poem—"Oncle Jules"—of my uncle running out from the safety of an underground shelter to the house in order to pick up the family's bottle of wine while the allies were bombing Marseille. [i.e. this seemingly mundane act of life and living [eating and drinking] fearlessly standing up to the un-sentient inhumanity of war.

Villon, François: Medieval poet. A "Charles Baudelaire" before his time, as a professor said. Villon expressed surprisingly modern angst in the middle age. [Reputed to be one of Bob Dylan's favorite poets].

INDEX

Titles in bold and first lines in italics.

ABOUT THE AUTHOR

Jean-Yves Solinga

Jean-Yves' family comes from Provence. He was born in Algeria, and lived thereafter between the south of France and Morocco in what he describes as an idyllic youth. Upon settling in America with his family, at the age of 15, he had already been writing poetry: being first published in *A Letter Among Friends* along with John Norman of New London, CT. After serving in the U.S. Army, he began a successful career in teaching and lecturing. Jean-Yves holds a doctorate in French on the representation of the Maghreban [North African] landscape found in the texts by Pierre Loti, André Gide, Albert Camus and Jean-Marie Le Clézio. He has published several books of poetry: *Clair-Obscur of the Soul* (2008), *Clair-obscur de l'âme* [in French] (2008), *In the Shade of a Flower* (2009), *Landscape of Envies* (2010), *Words Made of Silk* (2011), *Impressions of Reality* (2013), *Artist in a Pixelated World* (2014), and *Asymptotes at the Infinity of Passion: The Untouchable Quest of Poetry* (2015).

His books offer a singularly unique view of mankind's reflection through the prism of the lyrical language while in the midst of at times impressionistic poetry tackling many hard realities of history and society: Quoting Michael Linnard with "At times, some passages [that] are examples of the translation of the human condition into pure thought."

The author has been a featured speaker at the Alliance Française of New Haven and Hartford; Presented at the Center of the Teaching of French at Yale; The University and Southern Connecticut State University on the use of poetry in language studies; Published in "*Art et poésie*" edited by the renowned French poet Jean-Claude George. He has also read at the Poetry Institute of New Haven; Wesleyan University book store; the Cantab Lounge in Cambridge, the Blue Star Café in Providence, the Guilford Green Barn. He has featured at the Arts café in Mystic; the Hygienics; the Bean and leaf; the Bank Square Bookstore. He has co-featured at the Mystic Art Gallery, and at the Harriet Beecher Stowe Center on the theme of social justice in poetry. Jean-Yves has had poems published by the *Free Poet Collective Ekpharsis Project* at the New Britain museum, the *Ekpharsis Loft Anthology of Providence*, the *Little Red Tree Anthology*, the *Exquisite Project of the Bill Libraries*, and *Peacock Journal*.

His poetry has been nominated three times for a Pushcart Award. Jean-Yves Solinga is a poet of immense ability and range whose lyricism is truly remarkable. It contains many breathtakingly beautiful and sophisticated poems that reach out to the very limits of the human condition where true art exists. Many facets of his work find inspiration and perspective in his cultural duality. This gives his poems a personal as well as societal breath. In *Created Realities*, Jean-Yves explores the defused boundaries of the artist's life and his art.

Photographer by Andrea Keller

www.ingramcontent.com/pod-product-compliance
Lightning Source LLC
Chambersburg PA
CBHW080516110426
42742CB00017B/3132